Jason Cermak

TRAILER TRASHED

MY DUBIOUS EFFORTS TOWARD UPWARD MOBILITY

Hollis Gillespie

Illustrations by James Polisky

skirt!

Guilford, Connecticut
An imprint of The Globe Pequot Press

skirt® is an attitude . . .
spirited, independent, outspoken, serious, playful and irreverent,
sometimes controversial, always passionate.

skirt!® is an imprint of The Globe Pequot Press
skirt! is a registered trademark of Morris Publishing Group, LLC, and is used
with express permission.

Jacket design by James Polisky
Text design by Casey Shain

Library of Congress Cataloging-in-Publication Data

Gillespie, Hollis.
  Trailer trashed: my dubious efforts toward upward mobility / Hollis Gillespie ;
illustrations by James Polisky.
    p. cm.
  Includes bibliographical references and index.
  ISBN 978-1-59921-385-9 (alk. paper)
1. Gillespie, Hollis. 2. Journalists—United States—Biography. I. Title.
  PN4874.G385A3 2008
  973.92092—dc22
  [B]
                                                            2008018523

Printed in the United States of America
10 9 8 7 6 5 4 3 2 1

For my father—

"Ride with me," my father would say, and I'd hop in the car like a little bobble-head doll, not knowing where we were going but ready to warn him of upcoming police cars. He'd tell me of his dreams. He was gonna be somebody. On any given day he was gonna write a bestseller, become an inventor, or open a popular lunch counter. It was when he drove that his big dreams weren't overcome by bigger fears. So he drove, because if he didn't, then his demons caught up with him. If he didn't, then he would lie in bed, sometimes for days, and let his brain become his enemy. "Ride with me," he'd say. And off we'd go again to no place in particular. I went with him happily. I'd do it today with anyone else I love in the midst of our dubious attempts toward upward mobility. In the end it's not where you go but the ride to get there that matters.

The stories in this book are true so long as the truth can be trusted to my recollection (barring hyperbole and hallucination). Also, some names have been changed and events reordered. In fact, seeing as how certain memoirists are getting their asses ripped in half for fabricating elements in their books, I feel it's important that I finally come clean about a few things:

First—and please forgive me for this, because I know how important this is to my image—I was never actually, not in the literal sense, anyway (or any sense for that matter), a teenage prostitute to the stars. There, I said it.

But once Rod Stewart hit on me when I was 15. That's true. Okay, what really happened is that he hit on my friend, or someone who could have been my friend if I had, like, known her. Probably. And Lary might not be running a meth lab out of his house after all, per se. I'm not committing. And I sincerely regret anything I said that could have misled my readers into believing Lary is insane, including my frequent assertions that Lary is insane.

Contents

Hollis Gillespie, that's me

My Mother,
the missile scientist
with broken dreams of
becoming a beautician

My Father,
the trashed trailer
salesman

Milly, my magical daughter
who bestows her stuffed
animals with super powers

Cheryl, the crazy sister
who moved to Nicaragua

Kim, the good sister who
once punished her stuffed
monkey for cheating at
cards

Jim, the brother who
introduced me to
Led Zeppelin

Daniel, the talented
artist and sideline pet sitter
who can't keep his own
goldfish alive

Keiger, my on-again,
off-again boyfriend
who owns The Local
bar where I met Lary,
Daniel, and Grant

Cast of Characters

Lary, the event rigger who
insists he be the first person I
call if I ever wake up to find a
dead hooker in my hotel room

Grant, the bartender who once
offered to father my next child,
presenting me a choice between
young sperm from his old self or old
sperm from his young self

TRAILER TRASHED

The following are stories that recall my late father, a trashed trailer salesman who liked to bake cakes, and my late mother, the reluctant missile scientist he married, as well as the hard-fighting childhood they forged for me along with my siblings, Kim, Cheryl, and Jim. We would eventually scatter throughout the globe, and I, the true daughter of a traveling salesman, would become a career traveler, first for a failing airline and then stumbling to find my way without a corporate safety net.

On the journey with me are my three best friends, Lary, Daniel, and Grant; not to mention Keiger, the owner of the bar where we all met; and my daughter Milly, "the happy accident." I started collecting trailers because they reminded me of good family times. In the trailer homes of my childhood, for example, my father got to be proficient, my mother got to be impressed with him, and my sisters and I, at least for as long as the hookups were connected, got to buy the whole blissful picture.

1

///

THE FIRST TIME I FLEW, I WAS SEVEN and sick with a bad cold. Knowing now what I know about cabin pressure, I'm surprised my little head didn't explode like a frog with a firecracker up its ass and splatter the entire cabin with snot. It certainly *felt* like it would. Our mother, who was a little useless at conventional mothering, was commonly at a loss when her kids were sick. The most we could hope for was a show of odd courtesies—such as the time my sister got to choose the cartoons we could watch after she came home from the hospital after shoving a button so far up her nose it almost reached her brain—and this time, when being sick somehow afforded me special seating priority.

"Hollis is sick," my mother reminded my sisters, "let her sit by the window."

The flight lasted five hundred years, or at least it seemed that way. We were leaving to live in Florida, where my mother had scored work designing rockets for NASA. Until then, most of our nomadic lives had been confined to the state of California, which is luckily a very large state. In my seven years we had moved nine times, from northern to southern California, but nowhere in between, just lots of different places jumbled at either extreme.

Before our mother landed this new contract, we had been living in a somewhat dilapidated apartment project in Costa Mesa, and before that we had lived in a minor mansion on 17 Mile Drive in Monterey. As a contract worker building missiles and rockets for the government, my mother's income would ebb and flow in accordance with each administration. Either there would be a huge demand for bombs and rockets or hardly any at all, with our lifestyles inevitably reflecting either extreme and nowhere in between.

Right before we packed up to move to Florida, our father had been selling Silver Streak trailers at a big convention down at the fairgrounds. The Silver Streak brand was created as the affordable alternative to Airstream, though we couldn't afford one ourselves. Our mother was between contracts, and she helped decorate the different types of trailers. There were four, so she chose the four seasons as a theme. I remember the fall-seasoned trailer the best because she had sprinkled the small kitchen table with dead leaves.

Even at seven I questioned the aesthetic of dead leaves, but it was a motif that would stay with my mother for the rest of her life. Years later she decided to "go tropical" with our living-room interior by festooning the walls with giant palm fronds and circling bamboo place mats around a centerpiece that turned out to be a large ornate opium pipe she'd picked up at Pier One. This happened after we'd moved yet again, this time back to California, because when it came to locales it was always the East or the West, one coast or the other, and nowhere in between.

In the fall-seasoned show trailer, the kitchen table converted into a double bed after you dismantled it, dropped it down, positioned it to fill the space between the booths flanking either side, and evened it out by adding the cushions that formerly made up the backrests. In the end you had a bed as comfortable as a bag of Brillo pads, but our mother seemed to think this feature was amazing. Somehow the

Trailer Trashed

trailer slept six, though nearly all the sleeping areas required similar convoluted conversions before you could actually sleep in them.

"Really, it's simple," our mother would say as conversationally as possible to any passers through, "you just pull this out, push this up, and anchor it here. Isn't that amazing?"

Turns out what's simple for a missile scientist isn't necessarily so for anyone else, which might be one reason the poor man's answer to Airstream faded into oblivion with hardly a blip in the history of trailer consumerism. But until then our mother was trying like hell to help my father sell one.

On the trailer's kitchen table, in the middle of the leaves, she placed two carved decoy ducks. Our father's company folded soon after the convention, and none of the decorative accents our mother had personally provided the four show trailers were returned to her. Of considerable value, she complained, were the decoy ducks in the fall-themed trailer. She still lamented their loss even as she sat next to me on the plane ride to Florida, where she was due to start her new job and we our new lives. Again.

It made me remember our mother marveling at the many inward conversions the trailer was capable of in order to sleep six. *We were a family of six,* she joked. We could all live there. "Really, it's so simple," she'd say to customers, who scurried away like pampered cats avoiding a lonely visitor. They could sense her hope, I realize now, that if her husband could just sell a trailer, then maybe she wouldn't have to convert inwardly again in order to sleep a family of six.

Family Yelling

GROWING UP, I DON'T THINK I CAN REMEMBER a day I walked in the door of our house without being greeted with an outburst of some kind—and ducking. Ducking was essential, because you never knew what you were gonna get hit with. Once I got hit in the face with a wooden spoon covered in brownie batter, which my big sister, Cheryl, had hurled at me from across the kitchen (at that moment, she'd remembered that five years earlier I'd thwacked her in the head with a tennis shoe while she talked on the phone, which I'd done because, a year before that, she'd thrown a lamp made of deer antlers at me while we were visiting my uncle the hunter). So, both figuratively and literally, stuff was always swirling around our home. But at least yelling preceded it, so we wouldn't be caught unprepared.

But sometimes I was unprepared anyway. It depended on what was being yelled. Once I got yelled at for being late, which was really unexpected because I was always late. That was just something my family knew about me, and it had never garnered anything more than exasperation before.

That one day I walked through the door no more tardy than usual (which was the equivalent to complete punctuality, if you ask me). But for reasons that I cannot explain (except to say that they had something to do with my brother, Jim, falling out of a tree and needing to be rushed to the emergency room because he was bleeding out of his ear), I got yelled at but fierce.

It was not like my parents were even waiting for me, either, because they hadn't finished rushing around grabbing towels and whatnot to sop stuff up. My gray-faced brother was lying there on the hardwood floor of the foyer, having just been carried there by the father of the friend he was visiting when he fell out of the tree. Jim was shaking and spewing like a busted beer keg. He must have fallen far, I thought, because he did not look good. Then there was the blood coming from his ear, which had everyone yelling like panicked plane-wreck survivors.

After my parents wrapped Jim's head in a bedsheet, we all piled into my father's Corvair and sped to the hospital, with my mother holding my brother in her lap, which looked funny because by then he was twelve and almost as big as she was. When we pulled up to the hospital, the doctors made everyone back away so they themselves could pull his limp body with his bloody mummy head out of the car and carefully place it on the gurney; then they wheeled him through the swinging doors with my dad by his side. My mother stayed behind, standing there in the headlights of our car, her blouse covered in blood and vomit, wringing her hands.

When she returned to us, she noticed that my little sister, Kim, had peed in the backseat, which normally would have set my mother off yelling like a crazed street preacher, but instead she just sank to her knees outside the car door.

Curiously, she reached for us and gathered us to her like we were little life preservers in a rough sea, and held us that way for a long while, my sisters and me, even though we didn't, as a group, smell all that good. She didn't let us go until my dad came back to tell her my brother would be fine except now he was deaf in that one ear. "He's the same boy," he said, hugging her, "except now if we want him to hear us, we'll have to yell."

How to Carve a Bird

I DISCOVERED MEMORY THE DAY AFTER I STOLE a necklace from a friend's house. I was five and had pocketed the necklace while our parents boozed it up in the living room. Then when my dad got drunk enough to start insulting my mother in front of company again, it was time to go. The next day my mother saw me wearing the necklace and asked where I got it, and since I had not learned to spin effectual yarns just yet, I told a very ineffectual one instead, which my mother saw through like cellophane. Instantly she had my friend's father on the phone to say we'd be right over to make a big display of apology.

Lord, I did not know what the big deal was with the big display of apology. The necklace was just a charm in the shape of a small beer barrel on a thin silver chain, and even at five I knew that if you value something, you don't leave it sitting under the bed with cat hair clinging to it. And what's worse is that my mother herself was a complete klepto. She stole ashtrays from Sambo's coffeeshop all the time. We had them all over our house, with the logo of the little Nigerian boy being chased by a tiger. And our kitchen dish towel was actually a bath mat taken from Holiday Inn during our sojourn when we moved from San Fernando Valley up to Monterey, California, where my mother got a position developing computer systems after my father lost his last job selling trailers. But like all kleptos my mother kept her own credo: Only steal stuff from places that probably won't miss them until after you're gone, pretty much. (This is not exactly the memory I told myself never to forget, by the way; I just remember it anyway for no particular reason.)

Trailer Trashed

While we were there making the big display of apology to our neighbor, my little sister, Kim, who evidently thought she could fly, began to remove her blue turtleneck all of a sudden. "Fly, fly, fly," she kept saying. Turtlenecks, I suppose, are not aerodynamic. She had almost gotten it all the way off before my mother dove over the ottoman to stop her.

"Let her fly," the man laughed.

And that is the image I told myself never to forget, that of my mother diving over an ottoman to keep my sister from stripping, and our nice neighbor laughing and saying to let her fly. It just so happens that seconds before my mother dove over the ottoman, I'd had the revelation that I could make memories, and to demonstrate it to myself I swore I'd memorize the next instant forever. It has no significance other than it happens to be the first memory I told myself to keep after I realized I had the power to keep them. And once I discovered the power to keep memories, it was like I couldn't stop using it.

Afterward, our neighbor showed us his workshop where he carved wooden figurines. His specialty seemed to be the little birds that pop out of cuckoo clocks, because shelf after shelf was packed with these little wooden birds.

"Wow," my mother exclaimed reverently, which was unusual. I'd never seen her act reverently around anyone, but this man had been very gracious in the face of our big display of apology, so the least we could do was act impressed with his pieces of workmanship. My mother picked one up and said, "I could never carve a bird."

"Sure you can," the man said. "You just take a hunk of wood, visualize the bird in your mind, then cut away anything that isn't the bird."

This must have been meant to be a joke, because my mother laughed like she was watching *The Carol Burnett Show.* Then we went home and I never ever, not once, saw that man again, though years later I would find one of these birds in my mother's effects. I don't know whether my mother had sto- len it or received it as a gift, and she wasn't around to tell me. But I do remember that after the man told her how to carve a bird, she in turn told my father if he ever insulted  her again she'd leave him in the dust like a dead bush. They had a huge fight after that, but she stuck her ground. Sometimes I wonder if my mother hadn't learned to carve a bird for herself after all, visualizing what she wanted and proceeding to cut away anything that wasn't in that picture. *Let her fly,* the man had laughed. And my mother flew.

Trailer Trashed

Satan and Other Childhood Influences

WHEN I WAS SEVEN, MY OLDER BROTHER—who was not cool (he was the opposite of cool; in fact, if coolness were a sound wave, it would have to travel through several solar systems before it could even reach his outermost atmosphere)—brought home a Led Zeppelin album, which I listened to, because it's hard not to listen to a Led Zeppelin album when it's played in your vicinity.

I don't know what possessed Jim to buy the record. He was not into rock music. In fact, until the week prior, he had been an avid disciple of the Jehovah's Witnesses who lived in our neighborhood. Their coven mother had knocked on our door soon after we moved there and must have thought she hit a trifecta, what with my brother's youth, his impressionability, and the fact that our parents were going through a period of leniency in regards to our influences at that time. Our mother was in Washington designing bombs for the government. And our dad spent all his waking hours at the Tin Lizzy, a neighborhood bar he loved because he could walk in and holler, "Who's the head nigger in charge?" without his friend LeRoy the line cook throwing a punch, or at least not one in his direction.

Anyway, Jim was an avid Jehovah's Witness for exactly as long as it took him to learn that this religion precluded him from ever receiving Christmas or birthday gifts, which is something my mother, who was an atheist but not an avid one, made sure to point out to him while she was home on one of her breaks before she had to fly back to Washington and build more bombs. So the next time the Jehovah's Witness lady came to our door, Jim politely invited her inside and then incited my sister Cheryl to throw one of her famous volcanic fits—the kind where her eyes radiated lasers, her voice growled like she had a belly full of bees, and her spine coiled up like a cobra—and pretty soon the Jehovah's Witness lady was running from our house screaming about how Satan lived within our walls, or whatever.

So the next thing I knew, Jim brought home that Led Zeppelin album, and all I can think of is it probably had something to do with Satan living within our walls, because some of the boozers at my dad's bar said it was the devil's music. Even though my dad never listened to Led Zeppelin, he bought my brother a different album hoping it would influence him instead. So, in short, there was actually a time when, in our entire household, there existed just two record albums, one by Led Zeppelin 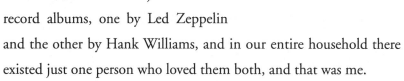 and the other by Hank Williams, and in our entire household there existed just one person who loved them both, and that was me.

The only thing I had to play them on was my sister's plastic Imperial Party-Time turntable complete with adhesive rainbow. The speaker consisted of one silver-dollar–size area near the needle arm with thirteen perforations—thirteen, which is sort of the symbol for

Satan, kinda—through which the music would waft with as much clarity as a corrupted radio signal. The volume knob was numbered to 13 (there it is again!), which was where I'd crank it and commence convulsing to the music. One time my mother returned from the airport to find that I had placed the turntable against our open window so the music could blare into our front yard, where my seven-year-old ass could be found before a thickening crowd, flailing to the beat.

She tried yelling at me to turn off the stupid goddamn music and get my stupid goddamn puckered poohole off the lawn and stop hopping around like a goddamn retard. When that didn't work, she could hardly move on to her natural next step, which would have been to hit me in the head with her shoe, because there were neighbors present and what would they think. So she walked right past me and into the house and unplugged the turntable, which caused me to simply stop and drop to the ground as though my puppet strings had been cut.

"She's being influenced by Satan!" a neighbor yelled.

Later my mother asked me what it was I loved so much about the music, but I was only seven and I couldn't explain how every chord seemed to reach inside me and inhabit my veins and awaken my limbs. I could not explain that to her; all I could do was want to explain it to her so bad that it must have measured heavily on my face, because the next thing she did was turn the music back on. At that I jumped up and shook my body while she shook her head as she made her way to the window and closed it to protect my ears from the noise outside.

Stairway to Seven

EVEN THOUGH I'M FAIRLY CERTAIN THAT MY FRIEND Lary is homicidal, I bet one of the reasons I keep liking him so much is that he sort of looks like Led Zeppelin's lead singer, Robert Plant. In fact, I think the first argument I ever had with Lary was about the Zeppelin song "Stairway to Heaven." It had been out for over two decades, and during that time I'd gone through seven stages of loving it and hating it and then back again, and Lary happened upon me during stage six, which was the strongest of the hate stages.

"Are you insane?" Lary hollered. "How could you hate Led Zeppelin?"

At that, of course, I had to refrain myself from impaling his curly blond brain on a rusty crowbar. Instead I exhaled and said with commendable evenness, "I did not say I hate Led Zeppelin, you total tampon. I said I hate 'Stairway to Heaven.' It's just a bunch of pretty words stuck together to get you to open up and let stuff in."

Lary countered with a passionate pro-"Stairway" argument, and normally I would have been surprised, because until then I thought Lary was only passionate about things like amateur taxidermy and objects that could detonate, but I was too busy reeling from having been accused of hating Led Zeppelin, when the truth is I had been a Zeppelinophile since I was seven. I used to lay my ear on the actual speaker of the plastic Imperial Party-Time turntable in an attempt to mainline the music straight into my brain—that's how much I loved Led Zeppelin. In fact, I did not just love Led Zeppelin; Led Zeppelin was my first love. Then when I heard "Stairway to Heaven," I loved it so much I begged my mother to pull over and stop the car because I craved a complete absence of any other stimuli that could compete with the sound of it on the radio.

I would call this stage one.

Then I took to singing all the words like I knew what they meant. I would interrupt my friends during our daily acts of pyromania to discuss the lyrics. "There's a songbird, see? And he sings in a tree by the brook," I'd pontificate. "And it makes me wonder." I would call this stage two.

Then seven years later I hated and feared the song because people were saying it contained hidden satanic chants, and at that time I didn't want to further tempt Lucifer, seeing as how I was certain he'd already possessed me after I accidentally read *The Exorcist,* which was sitting on my mother's nightstand. I would call this stage three.

Then I loved it again and ruined my turntable trying to play it backward so I could hear the satanic chants everybody was bloviating about in middle school. "I can hear it!" I squealed. But in the end you hear what you want to hear, and like any misanthropic preteen proud of her carefully cultivated sense of antisocialism, I wanted to fit in. "I can hear it!" I would call this stage four.

Then there was a long period where I simply detested the song with the force of fifty erupting volcanoes. It turned out that, after repeated inspection, the words meant nothing after all. The piper will lead us to reason *if we all call the tune?* "What the fuck does that mean?" I griped, inhaling my fourth Marlboro of the morning.

Evidently Robert Plant took a hefty tab of acid and ejected a farraginous pool of verbal vomit set to a smoking guitar crescendo, and everybody just foamed at the mouth and fell over each other in admiration over it. And what the hell is a hedgerow? This I would call stage five.

Then seven years later I didn't just hate the song, I was pissed at it. Not only did it disillusion me, it insulted me and made me loathe my impressionable younger self. I bought all those pretty words, didn't I? I swallowed it all, didn't I? The bait and the boat in one big gulp. Does the "dear lady" hear the wind blow? Does she know her "stairway lies on the whispering wind"? God, what bigger bag of bunk was there than these words? They were just there to serve as a wedge to get me to open up and let stuff in. Never again. *Never.* I would call this stage six.

Now my own daughter, Milly, will turn seven in a few years. She is the happiest accident I ever encountered. The most unexpected gift I would ever receive—testimony that alcohol mixed with indiscriminant sex has its benefits. Sometimes she sings along to songs on our CD player with such an absolute lack of insecurity that it reminds me there was once a time when I loved the sound of something so much I used to sit with my face fused to the speaker of a plastic turntable. So I love the song again, and the unrelenting crescendo of its melody, and sometimes I simply let it play over and over as I lie listening with my arms outstretched. The words are still bunk, but sometimes words aren't the point. Sometimes words are just there to serve as a wedge so you'll open up and let stuff in. And this is what I would call reaching the top of the stairway to seven.

Trailer Trashed

Winnebago with Wings

I HAVE RATIONALIZED THAT IT MAKES PERFECT SENSE that I work for an airline even though I am terrified to fly. For one, I'm certainly not the only flight attendant up there faking like everything is fine as we pass out Cokes three miles high in the sky. I, however, dropped the act around my coworkers after I figured out I couldn't get fired for my fears as long as I was fairly reliable about showing up to face them. Because of this honesty, other crew members are happy to let me sit in one of the jump seats that ensures my back is to the cabin so the passengers can't see the panic in my face as the plane ascends.

Still though, it makes perfect sense to me that I became a flight attendant. After all, I inherited wanderlust from my father, an inebriated trailer salesman who roamed the country trying to hawk his wares during his intermittent periods of employment. In between those periods he would describe his travels to me in such loving detail I'd dream of a livelihood that included travel as well.

Then, when I was sixteen, I fell madly in love with the bag boy at our local grocery store, who returned my affections up until the precise moment they interfered with his plans to live across the globe on an exotic beach under a lean-to and surf for the rest of his life. He made good on his plans, for a few years at least, leaving me behind like a little cloud of spent exhaust, with my heart as tattered as a war flag after battle. I never really recovered from being considered too unworldly to accompany him, and I think in that moment was born my mission to become the kind of girl he'd consider worthy. I spent years lost in daydreams about running into him during my world travels, the most popular being when I'd encounter him in some strange, far-off country, where I'd intervene just as the *polizei* were about to drag him to the hoosegow because of a misunderstanding that only I could correct because by then, of course, I'd be multilingual.

So I grew up to become an arguable facsimile of that fantasy image. And now I *am* a world traveler and a qualified language interpreter as well, embarking on my adventures by aircraft rather than by trailer.

Those glorious Silver Streaks my father sold were famously fashioned by aeronautical engineers after an airplane fuselage, after all, and an L-1011 is hardly more than a big, huge creaky Winnebago with wings. Also, at the moment my father died he was living across the street from the Los Angeles airport, with countless aircraft humming overhead in the thin air. At that precise moment, I happened to be in a small private aircraft humming overhead in the thin air as well.

Since that moment I've been terrified to fly.

But I do it anyway. And not just because I don't want to get fired. It's only fitting that I spend so much time on airplanes, and inside trailers too, because what is life if not a litany of attempts to relive our loves, correct our failings, and forge family out of thin air?

These days my family now includes Milly, not to mention my three closest friends, Grant, Daniel, and Lary, who have stepped in as surrogates for the small family I miss or I've lost altogether.

Grant is from Florida, even though that's hard for me to believe. I lived in Florida myself once, when I used to set fire to underbrush in all the undeveloped lots on our block, and when, at eleven, I reached the pinnacle of my pack-a-day cigarette habit and then forayed into marijuana use. Those were some good times, which causes me to think that Florida is full of a certain type of people, cigarette- and pot-huffing amateur arsonist type of people, and Grant is nothing like that. For one, Grant is way too fastidious. The Florida guys I knew were barefoot surfer boys. Grant, on the other hand, has sixty-seven pairs of shoes, and if he could, he'd wear each pair every day in an endless shoe-parade succession. There is just too much city in him for me to believe he's from Florida.

Daniel is from a tiny town in Texas located a frog-spit distance from the Mexican border. And even though Daniel wears designer sandals, there is still a certain sweetness to his countenance that makes it believable that his father is an avocado farmer and his mother a Wal-Mart greeter who sends him things like "The Famous Limited-Edition WilliRaye 'Boy Bunny with Backpack' Figurine!" When I look at Daniel, even though he now lives in a beautifully preserved mid-century modern split-level ranch with bamboo flooring and a built-in espresso maker, I can still see him sitting under the pomegranate tree in his aunt's backyard as a boy, barefoot in overalls next to his brother, feasting on fresh fruit while the big metal head of an oil drill seesaws in the background.

Lary is a complete social leper. He's supposed to be from upstate New York, though he keeps any evidence that he was sired from human loins as secret as possible. We didn't even know what he did for a living until recently, when we all were at the coffeehouse and heard him refer to someone as his boss. Grant and I looked at each other like we just heard Lary confess to a penchant for cross-dressing. Lary's *boss?* Up to then we never thought of Lary as having a boss. We always figured people just paid Lary to stick around or stay away, depending on their tolerance for a guy who likes to throw heavy equipment at police cars from the top of Philips Arena. He actually did that while on the clock once, but even then I never thought of Lary as having an actual boss. I swear I thought he just showed up with a tool belt and put his palm out like everyone else at the end of the day.

We infuriate each other, but we're family now. We are the water as well as the fish. No matter how many times we try to extract the hook, we will always get thrown back in. After all, we are in this adventure together, be it by wheels or by that big Winnebago in the sky.

Trailer Trashed

Trailer Trashed

My FRIEND DANIEL SAID HE CAN'T WAIT TO SEE how I'm going to dig my ass out from under this here third trailer I just bought. And he said it laughing, like he has any business being judgmental.

"Look who's talking," I sulked, reminding him that I don't have to take this from a guy who is so addicted to the home-shopping network he still has a year's supply of Lauren Hutton's tanning towelettes crowding his bathroom cabinets. "At least it's just my cabinet that is crowded," he said. "Where the hell are you gonna fit another old aluminum travel trailer? Your driveway is already full of old trailers. Your ass is now officially buried in trailers."

He's right. I will have to dig my way out of this, literally. Because digging, as it turns out, is the only way I can think to access my backyard with a trailer, as the easement alley that runs behind my yard has been closed up for years, fenced in by my neighbors on either side. So the only way I can tow a trailer through there is if I dig up a fence or two, and chop down a few young trees while I'm at it.

My other good friend Lary has already thrown up his hands, and he never throws up his hands. Normally he'd consider this a challenge, but the second I ruled out tearing down half my house, or those of my neighbors on either side—on top of vetoing a construction crane, when construction cranes are the subject of his wet dreams lately—he huffed out of here like an underbilled actress.

"Come back," I begged. "Look, here's some rusty barbed wire you can cut through."

But he was already gone. There was not enough destruction in the offing to entice him to stay. As he backed away, he barely missed the canned-ham camper I'd just picked up in Blue Ridge. "This place is like a damn trailer park," he bitched through his car window.

Ha! Like that's a bad thing. My dad often brought home demo models that were nicer than whatever hovel we were calling home that year. Once we lived two blocks from the beach in a clapboard cabin that had a toilet in the middle of the living room. Not a bathroom, mind you, but a single toilet, elevated even, as though on a throne, which I assume facilitated the flushing. It was not a very efficient use of space.

I now find it curious that we never actually lived in my father's trailers. Instead, they were a lovely reprieve from our actual home, and my sisters and I regularly found solace in them, where the deluxe roof-top air conditioner kept everything as cool as a mountain meadow. There, all the spaces and compartments were situated with perfect efficiency. Today's new homes are practically the size of monastery compounds, or at least airplane hangars. The humans inside wallow in the solitude this space affords them from each other, partaking fully in the distance—emotional and actual—that money can buy. When I think back to my father's trailers, especially now that I'm a parent myself, I realize there's a lot of comfort with the knowledge that— with a few tunings—an entire family could be happily accommodated in a thirteen-foot trailer. Everything you needed was there. Space was real space.

I recently moved into the tiny-ass house that I just bought, and I

Trailer Trashed

thought my daughter, Milly, and I would be on top of each other. But we're not. We're just close. That's how it is with the trailers, too. Just by virtue of their construction, by virtue of their efficient use of space, they bring the people who own them closer to things. Anything that does that is worth having.

"What about the last disaster?" Daniel reminded me. "Remember the 'free' trailer?"

Lord, he would have to bring that up. It's an incident I will never ever live down. Our good friend Grant will make sure of that. He will be five feet away from me for the rest of my life, ready with the evidence of my idiocy so he can slap me over the head with it the second I start to regain my confidence in humanity.

"'Free!'" is all he'll have to say. "'Free Delivery!'"

As if Grant himself were so impervious to scams on Craigslist. I remember he once used my buddy pass to fly to Jacksonville to buy a 1985 Volvo ("The two-door kind, just like I had in college!") from a young woman who said she had to sell it quick because she was starting an internship at a fashion magazine in New York the next month. He said he felt something, some slight poke in the gut the second he pushed the Send button on his PayPal account, but he brushed it off. The girl had all the components Grant looks for in a seller: rushed, naive, and nice. Grant gets most of his cars from people like this, then Grant—who is not rushed, not naive, and certainly not nice—relists the same car on the same site and sells it for twice what he paid.

But this time Grant got hosed. He stood curbside at the airport as she pulled up in the car as promised, only that was about the only thing that went as promised. The Volvo was a rolling wad of rust and Bondo because the girl, it turned out, had not used an actual photo of the actual car in her ad, but that of one taken twenty years ago. Then when she—all five feet, two inches and 300 pounds of her—opened the door and got out, Grant saw that the driver's side seat sat lopsided in the frame. But the car was his now and there wasn't much for him to do but get in and point it home for the six-hour drive.

"I'm sitting in a rusty shit pit," he wailed to me over the phone as he rumbled onto the interstate. "Gravel from the road is flying up through the holes in the floorboard. It's stinging my ankles! I'll never make it home. I think I smell carbon monoxide." I was laughing so hard I could barely hear him.

He made it home, and I still consider him the Craigslist master, though. He was the first person I called when I spotted the vintage 1964 Streamline trailer ("No rust! Well-preserved!") online for only $2,700. I jumped on it like a blue jay on a ladybug, just plucked it up and marveled at myself for being the first to stake my claim on such a find. "Bitch, look at this," I taunted Grant, attaching the photo of the trailer. "It's mine, mine, mine!"

"Girl, what the hell are you thinking?" he answered. "Where are you going to put a twenty-four-foot trailer?" This from a guy who once bought an entire truckload of old egg beaters to use as garden art. "Your ass is already buried in trailers."

"You're just jealous, you crusty bag of barnacles," I insisted, even though he was right. This was my third trailer, and since my backyard couldn't be accessed by trailer without demolishing the laundry room off the side of my house, they'd all have to sit in a circle out front like a little trailer park. I don't consider that a bad thing, but my neighbors might take issue.

"This one is a 1964 Streamliner in perfect condition, sorta, with working taillights and everything," I gloated. "It's a once-in-a-lifetime special opportunity because the guy is delivering it to me from Dayton for free."

"Ain't nobody doing nothing for free," Grant warned me. "Free ain't free."

So I called my sister Kim, an attorney, who happens to live in Dayton. I sent her as an emissary to pay the man his deposit. It probably took her two minutes to assess the situation. "It's a scam," she called to tell me with finality. She was leaving the locked lot where the trailer was parked. The "seller" had no key to the lot, but he did have a "purchase agreement," which, once signed, essentially entitled him to take a $1,000 deposit—in cash—on the trailer without stipulating any realistic obligation to deliver it.

When Kim pointed that out to him, he took very florid offense to her implication, but still refused to correct it. Further, he refused to produce a driver's license to show he'd be capable of transporting a 3,400-pound trailer 1,000 miles, or any identification at all that proved he was a legal party to the sale of the trailer. "So you saved yourself a thousand bucks," she said. "No charge for the attorney's fee," she laughed. "It's free."

Now Daniel is trying to talk me out of buying yet another trailer by suggesting there exists in my history a succession of mishaps such as this. "And what about the other trailer that you trashed?" he asked.

"That trailer was trashed when I bought it," I replied.

In fact, I *saved* that trailer like a neglected pet and found it a good home. It was a dilapidated 1974 Serro Scotty camper that happened to be too big for my trailer hitch—which I discovered when I looked into my rearview and saw that it had popped off the back of my bumper and was free-rolling into oncoming traffic. When I caught sight of that trailer rolling unattached along the highway about to cause a pileup that could depopulate half a high school, my heart stopped.

Thank God the trailer swerved into an irrigation ditch before it hit anything. I had to borrow Lary's truck to pull it out. Unfortunately the truck also came with Lary, and the ordeal cost me the entire supply of generic Peruvian Xanax I keep on hand for just such Lary-related bartering purposes. Predicaments like this make me wish my trailer-salesman dad had tutored me better before he up and died when I was young. It's true he'd stopped selling hitch trailers and had moved onto motor homes by the time I was nine, but he could have imparted plenty of wisdom in that time nonetheless. My mother taught me lots of stuff I remember perfectly well at that young age, like how to haggle the price down on a set of TV trays at the swap meet.

Trailer Trashed

"Tell her you only have twenty-five cents," she'd instruct me. "Say you want to buy them for your mom for her birthday." If I mentioned that her birthday wasn't for nine months, she'd remind me that it doesn't hurt to be prepared.

And she's right. Preparation does not hurt. I thought I was prepared with my tow hook on the back of my PT Cruiser, a car that Grant says proves I have lesbian taste even though I am not a lesbian nor have I ever tasted one. Well, it turns out that you can't tow a trailer that weighs more than your car, which, looking back, makes a lot of sense. But at the time all I saw was a 1974 Serro Scotty and all I could think of was how Disney World was opened only three years before this camper was built. My family, back when it was whole and we lived in Florida and both my parents were alive and employed at the same time, used to take a trailer like this one to a campground nearby called the Cozy Palms Trailer Court. There my parents would sleep inside while my two sisters and I would bundle in the same double sleeping bag under the night sky on the grass outside the door.

It wasn't the official Disney campsite, just one of those bargain ones owned by a chain-smoking retired forklift operator who kept his horny dog tied to a post by the check-in window. To my sisters and me, though, it was the Taj Mahal of trailer parks. We'd lie awake under the moon in a three-way spoon, counting stars and listening to the uncharacteristically subdued murmurings of our parents through the aluminum screen door. It's one of the few snapshots of immeasurable happiness from my past, and life is nothing if not a succession of stupid attempts to re-create those. Hence the trailers, trashed and otherwise.

Soon after that my father was gone and my mother's tastes went through a sophisticated phase, during which we lived in Switzerland and other hoity places. But in the end she bought a trailer because it turned out her needs were simple after all. I kind of consider that a blessing, to live long enough to understand that the human condition doesn't require a lot of luxury. I've traveled all over the planet myself since then, not to the Taj Mahal exactly, but I've stayed in other places that rival it in opulence while I was free-rolling through the world. In the end I bought a tiny house with aluminum awnings hardly bigger than the double-wides my dad used to sell. The backyard is big, though, and if you ask me it's begging for trailers.

Trailer Trashed

MILLY IS FIVE, AND I FIGURE SHE HAS BEEN FREELOADING long enough. Time to put her to work. She is a natural, after all. Nobody can resist her. When she brings her cupcakes to The Local, Keiger, the owner and bartender, doles out dollars to all his customers and extracts promises that they will each use theirs to purchase one. And the cupcakes aren't bad, either; they are cream-filled and fudge covered, encased in pretty pleated foil. MILLY'S HOMEMADE DING DONGS, the sign says. Yes, there is a sign. I made a sign. Got a problem with that? ALL PROCEEDS GO TO A FUTURE CAPITALIST'S EVIL PLAN TO RULE THE WORLD, it informs. So far she has made seventy-five bucks.

I was five, too, when I first went into cupcake sales. My sisters and I would go door to door with trays of the stuff. Once a neighbor wanted to buy our entire supply, but my little sister swatted her hand away. "Leave some for us!" Kim chastised her, and the neighbor lady did, but paid us for them anyway. I think that was when I discovered most adults won't turn down a kid selling cupcakes, especially if the kids have a good reason. I also discovered that lifting tidbits overheard from arguments between my parents worked really well in this regard.

"We're selling cupcakes on account of how my dad lost his job selling trailers again and we're gonna have to live on the streets," is one that worked.

"We're selling cupcakes to buy a monkey," is one Kim used to use, which also worked because she was just three and actually believed we were going to buy a monkey with our earnings.

The cupcakes were not our only product, and in fact we had a lot of opportunity to diversify during afternoons when we weren't playing air hockey at the bar where our father spent his days. The other products we sold were the ones he'd abandoned over the years in his many halfhearted attempts to garner an income between gigs selling trailers as we moved from town to town. The products would arrive in our home in boxes—which was convenient since we would inevitably be moving again soon, anyway—and that is where they would have stayed if we hadn't nosed around and found them one day.

What we'd found were boxes of greeting cards, wallets, key chains, and, oddly, chocolates (which, of course, we ate). We got a lot of rejection as we went door-to-door with the other things, but nothing sold as well as the key chains, thanks to Mr. Festerbeck, our five-hundred-year-old neighbor who used to own the paint store before he sold it to be torn down to put up a radiator warehouse. He never did buy anything from us, but he was always a hoot to harangue nonetheless. Plus he whistled through his dentures and had so much junk in his front yard it was like picking your way through a trove of tornado debris just to make it to his porch. But the most important thing is that the old man always took it upon himself to give us tips on our sales techniques.

"Stand by your product," he'd cackle. "You have to make me think I can't live without it. Like what's this? A key chain? What's so great about this key chain? Looky here, it clips to your belt and it's retractable! Well, my goodness," he'd exclaim, feigning wonderment, "think of the convenience! Think of the ease of use! Think of the bags of groceries

Trailer Trashed

that can be saved from being dropped on the front stoop all because of this magnificent key chain! All the cartons of eggs saved from being crushed. This right here will save you time and money! In fact," he gasped, eyes agog, "think of all the pretty ladies who get attacked on their front steps just because they took too long to find their keys in the dark of night! That's how you have to sell it; it can save your life."

And off we'd go, laughing, selling our Magnificent Lifesaving Key Chains door-to-door. We got more takers than we would have otherwise thanks to our kindly old neighbor, who, it turns out, could have used a lifesaving device himself. It wasn't long afterward that Mr. Festerbeck was found dead on his kitchen floor by the local exterminator, which explains why he didn't answer his door the last time we knocked. The exterminator had been hired by Mr. Festerbeck's neighbors as a kindly hint to rein in whatever it was that was causing such a terrible bug infestation emanating from his property, and the exterminator found the problem, all right. But when I think of Mr. Festerbeck, I'm careful not to remember that part.

When we ran out of key chains, it was back to the cupcakes because those were easily replenished. Occasionally my mother would dispatch my older brother to serve as a bodyguard on our salesman outings in case we knocked on the door of a child-molesting masturbator or something, which, looking back, was a questionable decision if you ask me. He himself was only twelve, and half deaf, and would not have served as a sturdy barrier between us and evil. But still my mother would holler at him to accompany us. "Your sisters could get kidnapped. Get your ass out there."

He was always reluctant to come, so to make it worth his while he'd invent reasons why he was needed. Once, as we approached the Gothic hilltop home of our strange neighbors, two sisters by the name of Blister, he told us that this here was where the kidnappers lived, the one our mother had warned us about. He then launched into a florid oration about the legend of the kidnapping Blister sisters, two women with wings like the pterodactyls that ate their own eggs in *The Land That Time Forgot,* and in spite of the fact that my brother had said they'd lock me in the crawl space under the staircase and feed me mice the rest of my life, I was excited to see the Blister sisters. I did not want to miss the sight of real live kidnappers, and considered becoming one myself. The wings, I tell you, were a huge draw.

The women who answered the door, though, did not have wings that I could see. They were tall and pale with their hair pinned in large white knots at the base of their necks. One had a bun the size of a bicycle seat. My brother was loitering at the end of the drive, behind the gate, out of sight and of absolutely no use should the kidnappers wield their hunting knives to gut us like little flounders. So my two sisters and I stood silently before them with our tray of cupcakes, quivering.

"What have we here?" one Blister sister asked.

"We're selling cupcakes—" my sister Cheryl began.

"Where's your wings?" I blurted. "We wanna see your wings!"

What happened next will remain one of the most vivid memories of my childhood, because damn if that woman's white bun did not, right then, come alive and spread goddamn wings as wide as the open sky. My sisters screamed so loud that lobsters in the middle of the Pacific were probably alerted to our presence, and ran back down the drive toward my brother, cupcakes in their wake. I remained there, though, agog. The bun had not been a bun after all, but a sleeping cockatiel. The lady let me stay for a good while after that, feeding the bird cupcakes, until finally my mother appeared at her door, dispatched by my terrified siblings to save me from the legendary kidnapping Blister sisters.

The Migration

I WONDER WHICH IS MORE TELLING OF MY GENIUS, the fact that I knew exactly where to get the two plastic asses, or the fact that I needed two plastic asses to begin with. "Girl," Daniel sighed, rubbing his eyes, "tell me again just what in the hell is it you're going to be for Halloween this year?"

"A double-butted baboon," I answered excitedly. "I already have the plastic asses."

"Of course you do," he said.

My genius is obviously wasted on Daniel, an artist whose gift is outside the double-butted variety. If you subtract the time he dressed up as a country-singing drag queen when he helped throw me my "Recovering Slut Baby Shower," I haven't seen him dress up in a costume since that Halloween a decade back when he was a priest with porn hanging out of his pockets. How he can let another perfectly good opportunity like the entire month of October go by without even at least gluing a fake bloody hatchet to his head is a mystery to me. But I don't judge.

"You pussy," I griped. "At least wear one of my headbands with the blinking bloody-eyeball antennae."

"Hell no, bitch," he griped back. "Don't draw me into your Halloween drama. I could injure myself. You practically get hospitalized every year yourself."

Please, the Halloween when I got the concussion was not even because of my own costume. I got hit in the head from the corner of a tabletop that was part of my friend's walking "Decapitated Head Served on a Platter" masterpiece. Of course, it might have helped if I could have seen through the black-lace veil of my evil-sorceress outfit, but details like that are secondary to the overall visual effect. Sure, I was blinded to the point of walking into oncoming traffic, but the important part is that my costume kicked ass.

It was my daughter Milly's idea for me to be the double-butted baboon. I won't tell you how she came up with the concept, except to say that grade-schoolers, as a matter of convention, are obsessed with anything ass-related. It's pretty much a time-tested fact. I remember when my big sister, Cheryl, was about that age. She used to pin me down on the bottom bunk and fart on my head before bed.

It's a shame they didn't have plastic asses for Halloween back when we were kids, because we certainly could have used them. Part of the reason I love to make costumes today is because I had scarce to work with when I was little. Cheryl and I both were expected, year after year, to wear the same butterfly costume we were outfitted with when we were in preschool and part of a parade float that spring. We lived in Pacific Grove, California, which is famous for being an annual migration point for massive hordes of monarch butterflies. I remember it was a big deal every year, to sit out on the porch waiting for the butterflies to return. We'd strain our eyes and pretty soon there they'd be, clouds upon clouds of them fluttering home. It really was pretty magnificent.

But still, for the first seven years of my life my Halloween costume was not even inspired by Halloween but by some bogus local butterfly worship. I swear, if I hadn't been so busy trying to squirrel away all the Laffy Taffy for myself, I would have crawled into the pillow sack of candy we collected every year to simply curl up in shame.

One October my mother cut the bottoms out of the little butterfly footies at the end of our little butterfly tights so our lanky legs could poke through and, hopefully, stretch out another year. Maybe it was the toes to the tights that poked out at about our knee levels, or the damn worn-out wings that were just about nothing but bare wire, but whatever it was she just stopped and seemed to understand it was time to get us new costumes. My sister and I could hardly believe our fortune. My mother stood by, bemusedly hoovering her hundredth Salem menthol, as my sister and I hooted all the way to the five-and-dime. We hooted all through the process of picking out the completely flammable, choke-hazard heavy death suits that would serve as our costumes that year, then hooted out the door on our way to gather our annual pillow sack of cancer-inducing, dye-laden sugar bombs. We were so happy we could hardly breathe.

As I bounded away, though, I remember stealing one single glance back at my mother. There she was, framed by our doorway, her head surrounded by a halo of smoke, her hand unsteady as she held the menthol to her lips. I know now what she was thinking. She was wondering when it was, exactly, that her little baby butterflies had gone and migrated away. She was thinking maybe she should sit out on the porch and wait for them to return. Yes, she'll strain her eyes and pretty soon there they'll be, fluttering home.

Trailer Trashed

No Ordinary Trash Pile

I RECENTLY SAW A BIG TRASH PILE on the side of the road and immediately thought of Daniel. It was no ordinary trash pile. Somebody's grandmother must have died or something, as no person with a passable knowledge of what's really valuable would have tossed half this crap onto the sidewalk. For one, there was a poodle-shaped toilet-paper cozy that was hand-knitted from pumpkin-colored yarn, and that is pricelessness right there, I'm telling you. There were also two fondue forks with Bakelit handles (broken, but still), a Pyrex candy dish, and almost an entire set of '70s ceramic dinnerware decorated with cute maroon mushrooms.

I would have jumped into it, but the pile was already in the process of being converged upon by a passel of culture vultures, and besides, I am simply not that brave. Once I was driving Daniel and his boyfriend, Mitch, along with our friend Gary around in my car, searching for junk piles. They found one all right, jumped out before I finished braking, and immediately started loading boxes of that musty stuff into the trunk of my car.

"What a haul! This is great!" they flittered excitedly.

"What the hell are you putting in my car?" I shrieked. "What is that, *maggots?* Are you putting *maggots* in my car?"

Sure enough, they were walking toward the trunk of my car with a pail of rotted old potholders teeming with maggots. "But these potholders are hand-hooked. C'mon," they insisted. I practically had to slam the trunk shut on their eager little fingers to keep them from pitching the whole mess past me regardless of my protests. The experience would have traumatized me for life if not for the fact that later that same day they spotted a yard sale in Cabbagetown that garnered me an original framed rendering by Jeff McNelly, the late triple Pulitzer-winning cartoonist. I spent five bucks on it and put it on eBay that night. Seven days later, the winning bid was so big I used it to pay for my ticket on a fourteen-day Hawaiian cruise. I am not kidding.

I still drive by that house sometimes, the one belonging to the man who hosted the yard sale. He'd dragged a load of old boxes out from the basement that had been abandoned there by the woman who owned the house before him, and he himself had owned the place for seven years. He was talking on his cell phone to his friend, complaining about the crappy turnout, when I handed him the ten-dollar bill for my two items. The other item was a vintage beer sign, the eBay resale of which just about covered my bar bill on the cruise ship.

Today, whenever I pass his house, I always whisper my thanks. I'd almost feel guilty if not for the fact that I myself have passed things up for trash in the past only to learn later they were valuable beyond measure. My mother once had an entire living room suite of vintage Lane furniture she bought brand-new in the early '60s, back when Lane favored a trim, teak, Danish-inspired design. I sold the entire suite for twenty-five bucks behind her back. Don't get me wrong, it was for sale anyway. My mother had advertised it in the paper, only she was asking way too much for it, I thought. So one day when she wasn't home, I answered the door and allowed someone to load it up for a fraction of its worth.

Trailer Trashed

God, do I regret that today. I remember that furniture moving with us from address to address in the house-hopping days of my youth, back when my parents were habitually outrunning the rent, each other, their own demons, or all three. The furniture stayed in pretty good shape, too, considering the abuse I personally put it through. There was an end table in particular, with clapboard cabinet doors, which I'd often crawl into and close up behind me. Sometimes I'd remain curled up in there for long periods, smelling the lasting fragrance of fine wood, eavesdropping.

It was there I was hiding when I heard my mother fall down the stairs, followed loudly by my angry father, who, it turns out, had pushed her. I forget what they were arguing about, but it sure was a roof-rattler. He wasn't done when she was finished falling, either. Not by a long shot. It was probably the longest period I ever spent curled up inside the end table. I wouldn't come out even after my mother finished crying, either, because I could feel the anger still there, weighting the air like dismal humidity. Finally my mother spoke, and I was surprised at how strong she sounded after having just fallen down the stairs and all. "If you ever, ever, goddamn lay a goddamn hand on me again," she said evenly, "I will throw you out like the goddamn trash."

It was then that they heard me whimpering inside the end table. They opened the door and tried to coax me out, but I wouldn't come out for a long while. Life wasn't exactly a bubblegum factory for us all after that, but my father never did lay another goddamn hand on my mother again.

The Tiniest Bit

WE WERE WARNED BEFORE WE TOOK OFF from Atlanta about the state of the New Orleans Airport, told to "prepare ourselves," as the entire B concourse had been converted into a rudimentary morgue. On the way there, a Federal Air Marshall further expounded that *morgue* might not be the right word. "*Dumping ground* is more like it," he said, as bodies had been simply shunted in that area, some still slumped in the airport wheelchairs that had been commandeered as provisional gurneys to get them there. Once we landed, it would be six hours before our people would be ready to leave. "You can wait here," he told me. "You don't need to go out there. The place is contaminated."

But upon arrival, I was the first one off the plane. I've always been that way. Even against my better judgment, I seldom pass up a chance to ogle catastrophe, dead bodies included. My own father's funeral was open-casket, and my mother graciously gave us, her teenage kids, the option of not viewing him in that state. "You can wait here," she said. I was the only one of my siblings who went in. I stood with him a long while, wondering if I could run my fingers through his hair. Finally I did. It was his hair all right, and I was surprised that his hair was there but he was not. In the end I wish I hadn't seen him like that; I wish my last memory of him could have been the last time I saw him alive, when he was making cocktail sauce, adding the horseradish very gingerly. "You just need the tiniest bit," he said. "The tiniest bit is enough. It flavors everything else."

He was from Birmingham, and he used to talk about New

Orleans like it was some kind of Emerald City, an enchanted wonderland. Even during his surprise last days, he used to constantly recount how he once saw Louis Armstrong at Preservation Hall. "You walk down the street," he used to say, "and you hear music coming out of every doorway. I heard that trumpet and walked inside, and there he was." It was like my father lived on that memory, kept it protected like a treasured talisman, and pulled it out often to ward off the harshness of a world that would relegate a man who loves music and the magic of New Orleans to an efficiency apartment and a job at a used car lot adjacent to LAX.

So when I was sixteen, I went to New Orleans and decided to stay a good while, moving in with my hotel's maid when I ran out of money. Her name was Shirley and she had an Afro like a perfect daffodil. One night I took her to Gunga Din's on Bourbon Street to watch the mangy drag queens insult the audience. That one tiny bit that I did—"taking her out on the town," as she called it—was enough to brightly color the rest of our relationship. After that she refused to charge me rent anymore. "You keep your money," she insisted, and I am still astounded by her kindness. On another day we walked through the French Quarter and stopped to listen to a child play the violin on the street corner. A crowd formed, and an elderly man asked Shirley to dance. He spun her through the street in beautiful, pitch-perfect ballroom maneuvers, his posture so erect and his face so proud, his steps so achingly graceful. In light of Hurricane Katrina, it is an almost unbearable memory.

That day the New Orleans airport was a lot like the city itself: dead but not dead, animated by oddities that should not be there, like the National Guardsman who pulled the Jetway to our plane, and the tented "hospital" on the tarmac where actual surgeries were performed, and the Red Cross workers, and the makeshift morgue. Most people had a gun or a badge or both, and those who didn't, the minority, were evacuees. They wandered aimlessly in clothes that were not theirs and, oddly, almost all of them were wearing brand-new baseball caps bearing industry logos.

I did not make it to the morgue because a truck had pulled up a few hours beforehand with a litter of sixteen puppies, which were each almost immediately adopted by disaster workers, who then walked them on improvised leashes throughout the atrium. It was probably almost the only thing that could have brought light into the eyes of these bereft people, and in the end that was worth seeing more than a makeshift morgue.

In all, it made me wonder about the world, the sorrow and loss, how lasting that is, how thick and insurmountable it seems, and then I saw puppies. And then I remembered how an elderly gentleman once danced in the street with a kind-hearted cleaning lady—held her in his arms like the perfect daffodil that she was—and I remembered the beauty of that, the aching grace of that, and suddenly I realized the tiniest bit is enough. The tiniest bit flavors the rest.

Trailer Trashed

Suitcase in the Center of the Freeway

THE OTHER DAY THERE WAS A SUITCASE SITTING in the center of the freeway, and cars were swerving every which way to avoid hitting it, not that hitting it would have been so bad. In fact, I wish someone had. It was just a framed canvas bag that might have gotten caught in your car grill for a bit but not done much permanent damage or anything. Still, though, people were giving it a wide margin. Traffic careened around it, people were late for things, and days were re-arranged. All because of a suitcase sitting there.

Christ, will somebody move that thing? I thought as I angled around it. I would have done it myself, but I had my child there to think about.

In fact it was her big day at performance camp at the Art Station in Stone Mountain, and when we finally arrived there, it was amid a last-minute panic to rewrite the play's script, because another parent had complained about the play's content, in particular the part of the "vestal girls," which was the little-girl equivalent to the vestal virgins of Roman mythology. The rankled parent had complained the part indoctrinated the young girls who played it into "militant lesbianism."

Personally, I think a vestal virgin is a much better role model for a little girl than the parade of infamous mini–crack whores invading the media these days; not that I have anything against mini–crack whores. I don't wanna judge. I know they must have mothers themselves, probably, and maybe those mothers burst with pride when their girls get out of a limo, for example, and angle those naked crotches so well for the photographers, or when their daughters' pupils are dilated so prettily in their mug shots. I just personally hope my girl grows up to aspire for more. But who am I? I'm just a parent actually there to see her child perform in the play, rather than a parent who was not planning to show up but nonetheless fired off an e-mail that had everyone engaged in the turmoil of rewriting the script.

"The vestal virgins were actually priestesses," I suggested, drawing from the memory of my own grade-school mythology classes, which, amazingly, did not steer me down the road to adolescent sodomy, eventual weapon-toting lesbianism, back-alley abortions, or death and the ultimate destruction of Earth. I did go through a bit of a pyromaniac phase, though, but maybe that's because matchbooks and cigarettes were kept in a candy bowl on our coffee table. I remember I was in a Christmas recital then, too, and my father missed every rehearsal, which was fine with me. I didn't want him embarrassing me by showing up all five-o'clock-shadowed and boozy-breathed, but when it came time for the actual performance, he was there in the audience, pointing his lit cigarette at me with pride. I do remember that. I absolutely remember that.

"In fact," I continued, "the vestal virgins were the only female priests in Roman mythology. So let's change the name of the part." So this change, among others, was agreed upon. The part of the chorus that included, "Do we get married? No!" was subtracted, because God forbid a little girl grow up to be independent and empowered outside of wedlock.

Trailer Trashed

43

No one thought twice before making the decision to rewrite the script, because any decision otherwise would have excluded the girl from participating, and in the face of decisions like this, it's always better to be kind than to be right. That is why I'm so impressed with the camp staff. This is "drama" camp, after all, and I can hardly think of a better way to equip your child to embark on life's journey than to bestow her with the flexibility to navigate the dramatic and circumvent the obstinate.

The girl was elated and the play went under way, with the new lines all the more hilarious for being mangled in their delivery. Afterward the ovations were made, the cake was served, the pictures were taken, and the parents were proud. Nobody mentioned the missing parent who'd caused the ruckus at curtain time. It was over. It was forgotten.

But on the ride home I thought about the suitcase sitting in the center of the road again, and all the cars that were redirected around it as it sat undisturbed, and how people can be like that sometimes, sitting undisturbed in the middle of everything, admonishing the chaos around them while obtuse to being the cause of it. I used to be the kind of person who would get out and move it, but now I just go around because I have this kid here to think about.

So as I drove I considered that Christmas recital when I was seven, when my jobless dad found the time to brush his teeth and tuck in his shirt long enough to sit in the audience and listen to me sing about the Virgin Mary and other militant lesbians. His proud face is what I was thinking about when we came across the suitcase again. It had been knocked to the side of the road, but other than that it was still sitting there, having gone nowhere.

A Straight Face

I DON'T REMEMBER MUCH ABOUT MY first-grade teacher except that she had a sweaty neck, yelled a lot, and used to throw chalk at us.

The year before, as a kindergartner, I could hear her screaming at her class all the way from across the blacktop, and I'd marvel at how loud the lady with the damp yellow bob could holler. The next year, when I walked into class on my first day of first grade and realized she would be my teacher, I tried not to grimace. I tried mightily to keep a straight face as I slouched toward my seat, but my countenance was as transparent as the promise of a politician. It wasn't long before my snarky towhead became the primary target for flying chalk.

Milly is in first grade now, and yesterday she brought home her weekly behavior report. It's usually a glowing testimony to her future as a national ambassador or something, or at least that's what I think, inasmuch as a series of smiley faces could be interpreted as testimony. Yesterday, though, I learned there was actually a repertoire of faces used to rate a child's behavior in first grade, among them straight faces.

"What's with all these straight faces on your behavior report?" I asked. All of a sudden my daughter's face, which is itself usually smiley, stopped to stare at me with eyes as large as lunar surfaces, her lip quivering, her lashes suddenly balancing two perfect teardrops like large liquid diamonds. This, folks, is my daughter's guilty face.

Her explanation, punctuated by precision-timed mini-sobs, basically laid the blame on a collection of culprits that included, but was not limited to, everyone else in the world, including Spider-Man.

Trailer Trashed

I knew she was waffling, but really, I thought to myself, they're just straight faces. It's not like they're frowny faces; God forbid she ever got a frowny face. If she ever brought home a frowny face, I might as well learn iPhoto right now so I could airbrush the prison tats out of our future family photographs. Then, in the middle of my own inner waffling, I heard her mention something about pushing a classmate by the "owl-pellet table."

An owl pellet is a dry wad of indigestible animal parts that has been regurgitated out the gizzard of an owl, and they're full of little bones and teeth and beaks and feathers and other awesome things kids love. Seriously, nothing is cooler to a first-grader than a big chunk of dried-out bird vomit, which might explain the eagerness with which the class gathered around the table, and might explain why my child pushed another child, and might explain why I thought for a few nanoseconds that kids will be kids and let's all go on with our straight-faced little lives as though nothing happened.

But I remembered an incident on a train when I lived in Zurich back when I was in my twenties and never thought I'd have kids at all, let alone care about straight faces. There were only four of us in the train, including a mother with her three-year-old and a green-haired heroin addict covered in so many piercings it looked like his lips alone had been impaled by the contents of an entire toolbox. I sat behind the mother and kept peeking with trepidation at the drug addict behind me so I could make sure to duck in case he had a mind to unzip his pants and urinate.

But it was the three-year-old who was the hoodlum. The little monster kept head-butting me from over his mother's shoulder. At first I said nothing, because surely she would do something to control him, but instead she simply cooed at him with soothing German murmurings that had all the effect of a gnat's attempt to stop a Mack truck. Then, get this, the boy spit on me. It was a sizeable loogie that landed right at the corner of my mouth.

Of course I had to say something, so I did, expecting the mother to at least throw the troll out the train window in admonishment or something. But surprisingly, she simply looked at me with the eyes of a vapid raccoon and said, "I don't believe in conventional discipline."

I was agog. What else could I be? Then the train stopped, and the heroin addict rose from his seat to leave, but before departing he stopped to stand beside us. I cowered, until thankfully his glare settled on the mother in front of me, and then—I swear this is true—he spit in her face.

"My parents," he growled as he turned to leave, "didn't believe in conventional discipline either."

So yesterday I made sure my daughter apologized to those she wronged. She continued to work the quiver-lipped and moony-eyed angle, hoping to turn me to her side, but in response—just as it was that time on the train all those years ago—I remained surprisingly resolute, considering the fact that it was all I could do to keep a straight face.

Trailer Trashed

Super Power

MILLY HAS A PURPLE BUNNY SHE BOUGHT from the Cathedral of St. Philip Thrift with her cupcake money. This bunny, she exclaims, has the ability to bestow super powers on people. Here is the process: She asks you to hold the bunny, which you will do because it's impossible not to, and she says, "Now you have your super power," and then she takes the bunny back.

"What is my super power?" you ask.

"You can run really fast," she'll say, or "You can fly," or "You can jump really high." My own personal super power that the bunny bestowed on me is the ability of super strength, "like you can lift the whole world," Milly says, but sometimes that power doesn't sound as fun as flying or jumping really high.

"I don't feel really strong yet," I complain, but Milly tells me the power will come when I need it.

I could have used it the other day, I tell you. The two of us plus the purple bunny were in Washington, D.C., walking along the massive courtyard that connects all the Smithsonian museums, taking pictures of each other that optimized the images of monuments in the background. I took one of her that made it look like the Washington Monument was sprouting right from the top of her head, and she took one of me that made it look like our nation's Capitol was perched in the palm of my hand, which could serve as testimony to my super strength if I ever need testimony of that. It was about five hundred degrees Fahrenheit outside, and if my super strength had kicked in right then, I would have used it to spin the giant Calder sculpture in front of the National Art Museum so fast it would have served as a fan to cool off the entire world.

We were on our way to the insect zoo at the Natural History Museum because my girl loves insects—the bigger the better—and spiders, too. At home I'm forbidden from kill-ing spiders, all of which she has named. She can hold a Madagascar hissing cockroach in her hand like it was a little pet. She'll giggle about how all its hundred little cockroach legs tickle, while I try to muster the super strength to keep my skeleton from ripping itself free from my skin and scuttling into the corner where it wants to cower in repulsion. But Milly wants to be an entomologist, and when your child, who is barely out of kindergarten, tells you she wants to be something, especially if it's something you yourself have to look up in the dictionary, then you better muster up some flight benefits and get your insect-phobic ass on the ball to steer her where she needs to go.

The insect zoo was for my sake as well as hers, because she already knows way more about them than I do, so I was hoping I could bone up on insect awareness while the insect-zoo "handler" deposited all these massive specimens into my child's hand. At one point I turned to see her holding a grasshopper bigger than a bird and more colorful than a tropical sunset. "It's luminescent," Milly said, and I thought,

Jesus God! Where did she get that word? Then I remembered I'd used it to describe to her a large opal ring in the display window of a jewelry store once, and damn if that grasshopper didn't look exactly like it had been painted with about a million miniscule opal stones. I almost wanted to touch it myself after that.

Later, while walking back to the hotel, we stopped at the cafe in the sculpture garden, and as I fortified myself with liquid for the trek through desert heat, Milly passed her purple bunny around to the other patrons, bestowing on them each their individual super powers. She announced proudly that her own super power was the ability to become invisible, and to prove it she asked us to close our eyes for a few seconds, which we sort of did, and then when we opened them she was gone. "Do you see me?" we could hear her ask from behind the Lichtenstein, which prompted us to exclaim to each other very loudly, "I hear her, but I don't see her! How amazing!" And then she would ask us to close our eyes again, and when we opened them, there she was again. Amazing!

Later, when the other people had gone and it was just me and my girl, she looked up at me and informed me that she was going to demonstrate her super power right there in my lap. "Close your eyes again," she said, and I did. "Now open them," she said, and I did. "Am I fading?" she asked. "Am I disappearing?"

Just then—looking at her lovely face, at her eyes so large I could see in them the life I almost had without her, how less luminescent that life would have been, her eyes so big and beautiful and unbearable—all of a sudden I was desperate with hope that my super power would come to me immediately. I need all the strength I can get. Because she is right. She is disappearing. My little girl is disappearing before my eyes.

Uncorrected

I REMEMBER THE PRECISE MOMENT my father's heart stopped beating. I was in a small aircraft over Orange County, a four-seater Cessna that was getting tossed in a storm like a bathtub toy in a Jacuzzi. My roommate John sat next to me, a pound of cocaine between us, and he behaved surprisingly pussy-like for a pusher. He put his head in my lap and cried the whole way, certain we were bound to die horribly. I was certain we would not, but I didn't like him much so I let him cry uncorrected. When the clouds cleared, I remember looking at the lighted landscape below and thinking the formation reminded me of a skull. Wouldn't it be funny, I thought, if that meant something? Weeks earlier, on my academic calendar hanging on the wall at home, I'd drawn the image of a skull on this very day, in anticipation for a scheduled biology test I was certain I'd fail. In the end I skipped the test and hopped that impromptu plane ride to Los Angeles with my drug dealer roommate instead.

It hurts my heart to think about that, just like it does to think of Daniel's heart hooked up to wires like a coma patient. Mind you, I have no idea if coma patients are commonly hooked up to wires; it just seems like they should be, you know, in case their heart stops beating or something. I have actually been near someone whose heart stopped beating once, someone who was not in a coma, someone who was just standing there in the aisle of an aircraft, and you would not believe the ruckus a person can make when that happens. They flail around and flop on the ground and knock things over, and it's pretty obvious to everyone around them that something is wrong. They certainly don't need a wire hooked up to them to alert others at that point, whereas if they were in a coma, now, they would probably not flop very much at all. Their heart could just stop with hardly anyone noticing.

Hence the necessity for wires. Ever since Daniel was diagnosed with HIV a few years ago, I have been offering to fill his prescriptions on my layovers in Peru and on my visits to my sister in Nicaragua. I have also offered to go to support groups with him, but he walked out halfway through the one and only session he ever attended and refuses to go back. "Too negative," he'd said, which I found ironic, since the point was to be positive about being positive. But in the end, whatever Daniel is doing seems to be working, because to be with him you'd think his condition wasn't an issue. But then there comes something to make it crash to the forefront. Like his recently being hooked up to wires.

All I can do is ask him if he needs anything, and it's rare when he says he does. Lately I've been swapping my trips to Frankfurt in order to work the flight to Peru instead, where the pharmacy is right next door to our layover hotel. Normally, as a German interpreter, I would never work a flight to Central America. But things change. For one, these days the airplane nightmares hardly bother me at all anymore. I started having the dreams years before the airlines hired me, which is a fact I never really calculated until I was sitting there in the job interview. "Do you suffer from recurring dreams?" the interviewer asked me.

"None whatsoever," I said, realizing it had been eight years since I'd slept soundly without the aid of alcohol, sex, and/or narcotics. But

Trailer Trashed

I comforted myself with the realization that technically the dreams weren't really recurring—were they?—as the dreams were always different; it was just their theme that was the same, the general topic being a plane falling from the sky with me either in it or on it or under it. That's all.

"That is what we'd call 'recurring,'" said Daniel.

Thanks to an industry perk called buddy passes, Daniel sometimes gets to go with me on my drug-running exertions. He was with me that time the pilots aborted landing while we were flying home and I practically cut off his air supply, I was clinging to him so tight. Screaming, too, and you'd be surprised at how people just take screaming in stride on an aircraft. I personally think it ought to draw more attention, but I'm glad it didn't in this case. I might have been recognized later while in my uniform serving some of these same people on their connecting flights.

"You're gonna be fine," Daniel kept telling me, but not loud enough for me to really hear him over the loss of my own sanity. I seriously hate aborted landings more than almost any other cockpit mess-up I can think of. When your plane is within a few hundred feet of the ground and then, rather than land, it takes off again, it upsets the entire delicate ecosystem of comings and goings put into place by the control tower, because suddenly a plane that's supposed to be on the ground is thrust back into the rotation instead, which requires tons of frantic repositioning of other planes up there to make room. Every time I'm on a plane that aborts landing, it's all I can do to keep from shrieking like a fishwife.

"Shut up, bitch," Daniel tried to tell me. "Did you not hear me say you're gonna be fine?"

I did not hear him. I was too busy envisioning midair collisions and my pancreas impaled on a patio umbrella. I was already mocking the God of crappy luck just by being on an AeroMexico flight to begin with after I'd sworn to boycott them because of that crash in Mexico City in the '70s. But then Daniel got sick and the crap-ass place where he works won't provide him decent medical coverage and AeroMexico has the unique quality of covering more Latin American routes than my airline while honoring my pass-rider status. So I give Daniel my buddy passes and we make these side trips together because pharmaceuticals are so much cheaper down there, plus if you get the right pharmacist he is not picky about prescriptions, which can be a pesky detail.

"You're gonna be fine," I keep telling him. "We should go to Peru next, because you can buy bootleg movies there for a buck. And we have not even begun to tap our Nicaragua connection yet."

We finally got on the ground after the aborted landing that scared the holy hell out of me, and Daniel was rubbing his fingers because I had mutilated his hand by squeezing it so hard. "Look at this, I've got a lobster claw," he complained.

"Shut up, bitch," I said. "Did you not hear me say you're gonna be fine?"

I teased him that this is proof he'd do anything for attention. "Always fucking grabbing the fucking spotlight, fucker." I said, because I tend to spout profanities even more than usual when I am

Trailer Trashed

heartbroken. For example, the day my brother-in-law Eddie called to tell me my little niece almost got crushed by a roll-away car, her little liver lacerated by her own ribs, all I could do as I flew to the Phoenix hospital where she'd been airlifted was sit in my seat, clutch my head, and whisper, "Shit. Shit. Shit." The other flight attendants patted me on the shoulder, insisted I drink some water, and told me my "nephew" would be fine, that God would take care of him. Since all I could do was cry and cuss, I never told them it was my niece, actually, who was hurt and it was God, actually, I held to blame. Soothed by their voices, though, I let them speak uncorrected.

Regarding Daniel, I try not to act like it's any big deal, his condition, but sometimes it hits me all of a sudden, the probability, and I am frozen for a bit. I swear my own heart stops when I think about it, so I try not to too much. But when he is joking about his wires, like how he's going to take them off himself and put them on his fat house cat, Jenny, and let the doctors decipher that, the panic creeps in and I just can't bear it. "You goddamn pussy," I respond loudly, laughing loudly. Everything loudly, as I have inner sounds of my own to drown out, like the sound of that Cessna engine so long ago.

"Doesn't that look like a skull to you?" I gleefully tormented John, pointing out the window of the plane. "Look, the sign of death. Could it be a bigger sign?" I smiled inwardly as John whimpered and the plane continued to lurch. Since then I've been on over a thousand flights, and this one still marks the most turbulent. It also marks the last time I was unafraid to fly.

The next morning I learned my father's heart had stopped the night before and no one was there to hear the ruckus he made, no wires attached to him to alert anybody. His heart just stopped with hardly anyone noticing. For months afterward my freshman-year college roommates made much creepy ado about the stupid skull I'd earlier drawn on my calendar on that very day. John, in particular, thought there was some otherworldly reason for the image I'd foreshadowed on the day of my father's death. "She knew," I could hear him whisper to my other roommates. "She saw the sign of death."

I remember thinking it would be great if that were true, if there really was a wire that connected us to a reason for things, even if it's just a reason for why we search for a reason when there is none. "Really, she knew," I could hear them whisper. In response I simply lay in bed, bereft, letting these people believe they found a reason for something, letting them continue to talk uncorrected.

Trailer Trashed

An Amazing Feat

WHEN I WAS FIVE, MY BIGGEST TALENT WAS SHOPLIFTING at the local Thrifty drugstore. At first I just stole candy. Charleston Chews were my favorite, but their long shape made them hard to heist, so I developed the masterful trick of stuffing things into a rolled-up beach towel. It worked great until I got greedy and graduated from Charleston Chews to Slinkies, then to kites and then onto entire sets of Tonka trucks. By the time I tried to leave, my beach towel was so stuffed it looked like I was trying to transport a corpse in a rolled-up area rug. I got busted, of course.

"Where's your mother?" the store manager asked me.

"She's at work," I said.

"Then where's your father?" he demanded.

"He's at home asleep," I said, and even though it was three in the afternoon, I probably wasn't lying. My dad napped a lot during his bouts of unemployment, probably due to the increased voracity in his beer consumption at these times, which is one of the reasons I was so deft at escaping the house in order to shoplift at the Thrifty store. My two sisters were probably, at that moment, trespassing onto the property of the small motel across the street from our house so they could swim in the pool, and my older brother was engaged in who knows what horn-dog activities common among post-adolescents. The last place any of us could be found was at the forefront of someone's mind, it probably seemed.

"Well," the store manager exclaimed, looking at me with an odd judgmental sympathy, "if your father wasn't worthless, he'd be ashamed of you," he said as he ushered me to leave. When I got home I was relieved to see that my father was not waiting on the other side of the door like I'd worried he'd be, all freshly informed of my thieving, slapping his belt against his palm, growling. Instead he was—I swear this is true—baking a cake.

This was another way he spent his time during his bouts of unemployment, and I loved his cakes. They were amazing feats. He used to let me pick out the kind I wanted by pointing to the pictures on the mix boxes ("The brown cake with the beige frosting, and stacked up, not flat!"), and I was always amazed that they came out looking relatively similar to their advertised images. I didn't know not to be proud of my father until that day I got caught shoplifting by the Thrifty store manager, and I didn't know my father's pride in me could be so important that the thought of losing it would make me quake for days after I got caught, not sure which I feared more, that the Thrifty manager might track me down and tell my father to admonish me for what I'd done, or track my father down and admonish him for what he'd allowed me to become.

As the days wore on, my mother continued to go to work and my father continued to bake his cakes and take his naps and deal with his circumstances as best he could, and my siblings and I continued to wander so freely and so far from home that sometimes I'm surprised we survived, seeing as how kids are considered downright endangered these days unless they're raised under surveillance like lab mice.

Trailer Trashed

But we did survive, and became business owners, executives, and parents ourselves. I stopped shoplifting that day I got caught, because say what you will about my unemployed dad, the fact is he had made his pride in his children matter more to me than my klepto ways, no matter that my own pride in him noticeably waned after hearing him called worthless by a drugstore clerk. Today, though, I am more attuned to the fact that parenting is as painful as it is almost impossible. People are rife with insecurities and inner demons, and sometimes it's all they can do to protect their kids from their own crumbling opinion of themselves. To raise a child, let alone four like my dad did, amid this inner and outer turmoil is, quite literally, an amazing feat. I used to wonder if, had he lived, my father might be proud of me today, seeing as how our parenting styles turned out to be so contrary. Lately though, I spend less time wondering how proud he'd be of me and more time amazed at how proud I am of him.

Crazy (Is) Relative

MY MOTHER DIED BEFORE SHE EVER went completely crazy, but she was *relatively* crazy and also incredibly strong-willed—which explains why I'm never completely alarmed when I hear screaming coming from next door. It turns out my neighbor, Dolly, is not at all accustomed to being attacked by her mother. In fact she's very put off by the whole experience.

"I tell you I have had the worst couple of days," said Dolly. "She thinks the house is full of strange babies, and yesterday I caught her trying to escape down the street with the dog in her arms."

Dolly's a good neighbor and hardly ever imposes on me, considering she lives with a person in the throes of dementia. If I were in her situation, I'd probably be a lot more intrusive on the surrounding households. And for an eighty-five-year-old woman suffering advanced Alzheimer's, Dot is still pretty deft at keeping the craziness within the walls of their home—or Dolly is good at secluding it there. Only a few times have I ever had to usher Dot's barefoot, nightgown-clad butt out of the street and back to her doorstep.

Take that time I caught Dot in the middle of the road collecting industrial material that had fallen off the back of a truck. That did not seem crazy to me at all, except that it was 60 degrees and Dot was wearing one of those '50s-era, Lucille Ball–type ruffle-neck negligees. But it's not like it was the first time someone rushed out of the house in their pajamas to deal with a dire situation. I remember a man did just that once when I was seven and I'd found our dog Bonnie stuck butt-to-butt with some mutt up the street. I bawled sorrowfully in my ineffectual attempts to pull them apart until a man in pajama bottoms, obviously roused from sleep, took it upon himself to save me by throwing a bucket of cold water on the dogs, which caused Bonnie to pop free and commence gestating the seven puppies she'd have a few months later. I did not think that man was crazy at all, just a Good Samaritan.

So that's what I thought about Dot when I saw her in the street that time, collecting hose valves and coiled piping that had fallen off the truck. To me it all looked easily dodge-able until the person who lost it would discover it was gone and retrace their route to retrieve it. But Dot insisted on clearing the road that instant. I led her out of the street and finished moving the debris to the side of the road myself, with her pointing out where I missed a spot, even though I didn't miss any spots. I didn't think she was crazier than me, just more thorough. Crazy, after all, is relative.

Dolly admitted her mother to a treatment facility the other day, the screaming and histrionics having reached a point that was intolerable for her, especially after Dot took to insisting Dolly was a dangerous stranger who'd kidnapped her (long-dead) husband and real daughter, hence all the attempts at escape lately. I'd just seen Dot out and about, and she didn't look like she was plotting an escape. She looked comfortable, tottering around in her pajamas. *I can't wait to get old,* I thought at the time, *so I can wear whatever the goddamn hell I want and dance a jig in a rain shower if I feel like it.*

Though I have always known Dot to be cantankerous, it's only been a year since we met, and according to Dolly, all this screaming and viciousness is not Dot's normal self. So I can only imagine what it's like for Dolly, constantly dodging attacks from this little old lady living in her house, who happens to be her mother, accusing her of kidnapping her younger self. How hard it must be, I think, to hear your mother wail for the child that you were, to look at you as though you are a stranger, as though we don't all miss our younger selves enough as it is.

My own independent mother used to tell me all kinds of things about myself I didn't believe. She used to marvel at how strong I was, and I thought she didn't know me, because most of the time I felt more helpless than a hermit crab without a shell. I used to look in the mirror and wonder if she was confusing me with herself. I used to think she was a little nutty for seeing herself in me like she did, but again, crazy is relative. The late novelist Sheila Ballantyne once said, "You can always trust the information given to you by people who are crazy, because they have an access to truth not available through regular channels." So maybe Dolly did kidnap her younger self—don't we all eventually? —and maybe my mother was onto something as well. Because lately, I swear this is true, when I look in the mirror these days, I sometimes see her strength looking right back at me.

Hookups

I'M DYING TO SHOW MILLY THE KEY CHAIN for our new (or newly purchased old) trailer. It has a tiny Formica beer mug attached to it. I remember that my own dad never used to lock the doors of his trailers and motor homes, which probably explains the ease with which his last one was towed away when the repo people finally found it. My dad discovered the trailer missing after his daily beer-belting marathon at the local tavern, and he was only half as pissed as I thought he'd be. In fact, he was more mad the night I broke the seemingly less valuable Stan Laurel half of the Laurel and Hardy plaster statue set he gave my mother on her fortieth birthday (*that* night my mother had to fling herself in front of me because my father had his kicking foot all drawn back and poised to land on my ass).

The night the trailer "went missing," all my dad did was call me and my sisters outside, point to the empty carport, yell at us about how the trailer was taken "right out from under us," and ask us why the hell we didn't just lie down in front of the tires to block the evil repo men. But I think he went easy on us because he could tell from our faces that we were more bereft that the trailer was missing than he could ever be.

For one thing, it meant no more camping, and to us camping meant something entirely different than it does to most people. To us, camping meant parking ourselves at a vast concrete lot where trees and wildlife were about fiftieth on our list of priorities, way below the really important stuff, like amenities and "hookups." In fact, it was possible, if you worked it right, to not lay eyes on any actual nature for the entire trip. You could just spend the day sitting next to your trailer in the concrete RV lot, swimming in the concrete RV-lot pool, then playing billiards in the concrete RV-lot clubhouse. This was paradise on wheels. One time the RV-lot amenities included a diner where you could make your own pancakes on grills in the middle of the tables. At the very least, amenities meant a snack bar during high season, vending machines for the off months. When our mother showed us brochures for consideration for future trips, we would ask, "Are there hookups?" because to us the term "hookups" had come to refer to everything, not just the plumbing and electricity but the entire concrete wonder that RV camping had become.

"There's a waterslide!" she'd exclaim, and we'd all squeal with excitement, my father included.

Because it was my father who was in charge of all the hookups. There was a panel along the side of the trailer with big outlets behind it that he attached things to, which magically enabled us to do a wide variety of things that weren't nearly as amazing at home, from cooking sausage links to flushing toilets. My mother would actually show him affection, because in our real home, where my parents customarily fought like rival tigers, my father was not nearly as proficient as he was in the miniature-trailer version of our home. In the miniature-trailer version, everything was compartmentalized, cleaner, newer, and more manageable. In the miniature-trailer version, my dad was in charge and my mother was enamored with him and my sisters and I basked in the entire harmonious mirage of it all. Look at us, a happy family.

Trailer Trashed

I purchased the vintage Shasta trailer without really thinking about particulars, such as towing the damn thing home. I thought maybe I could have it hauled here and sit it in my yard as a lovely restored relic or something. But my daughter bought the whole har- monious mirage from the moment we started researching travel trail- ers on the Web. To her, the purpose of the trailer is not simply to plunk it somewhere in order to make a fun statement. To her the trailer is paradise on wheels.

"Where are we taking it?" she asked excitedly. "Disney World?"

So I started thinking maybe I could tow the damn thing myself. I had never towed so much as a red kiddie wagon with this car before, but I got a hitch put on, and damn if that little Shasta trailer didn't tow like a (kinda wind-resistant) dream all the way back from Indiana. I would not have believed it possible if not for my girl. That's one of the surprise perks of parenthood: When you have kids, you get to believe everything all over again. I can't wait to see her face when I show her the trailer. "That right there," I'll say, pointing to the panel on the side, "is where you put the hookups."

THE GOOD SISTER

Growing up, we drifted to so many addresses that often the only people my sisters and I could count on as friends were each other. Jim was old enough to move out while we were still in grade school. But my sisters and I are almost exactly twenty-two months apart in age, a fairly perfect gradation in maturity for being best friends throughout childhood . . . only to go on drifting, apart and then back together again, through marriage, parenthood, and other various estrangements. My little sister, Kim, sees the good in everything, which I used to find exasperating. But then she recognized goodness in a young, drunk, part-Swiss, part–South African who dressed like Crocodile Dundee—and she married him. My brother-in-law Eddie turned out to be my unexpected savior when I attempted a nearly disastrous foray into real-estate investment after finding myself abruptly unemployed. Therefore, I believe, if Kim sees the good in something, then the good must be there.

"God" with Two Syllables

I CAN'T PINPOINT THE EXACT TIME WHEN my sister Kim got right with God, except to say that maybe she always was. It's true that she never seemed to go through that phase where she did drugs and fucked around like her other sisters—me, admittedly, and my older sister, Cheryl, not so admittedly—but it's not like Kim carried a Bible around and spouted Scripture, either.

For one, if she did that my mother might have parked a roll-away bed on the balcony and demanded she live out there until it was time for her to attend college. It was tough enough, I know, for my atheist mother while we were young, when my dad would belt one too many Budweisers and break open the hefty children's Bible we still kept hidden in the bottom drawer of the big room divider. He'd insist we gather around and he'd read to us in his James Earl Jones voice. After a few minutes our mother would attempt to save us by distracting him with the sound of air escaping from another can of opened beer, and it sometimes worked. Other times, though, he would go on and on, hyperpronouncing the "d" in "God" so the word sounded like it had two syllables: Ga-duh!

But maybe some of the Bible stuff got through to us. Personally, I can't say it really manifested itself any further than the fact that, as a child, I was terrified little devils would claw through the underside of my coffin after I died, grab my dead heathen ass, and perform cunnilingus on me for all of eternity. I realize now that hardly paints a picture of hell, but as I got older my fears became less fun and more sophisticated, and I began to dread the day Rapture happened and my good sister would get sucked up to heaven and leave me alone with the pagan flotsam that comprised the rest of our family.

Because try as I might—and truthfully, I didn't try that hard—I was never as good as Kim. She seemed to have been born with an abundance of intelligence and integrity, and maybe we're all born with this, I don't know, and maybe it's a matter of simply keeping it intact, as if that were so simple. Whatever it is, Kim had it and I didn't. Don't get me wrong, I never agonized about this beyond the thought that, if there were to be the big prophesized divide one day between good and evil, Kim would be on one side of it and I'd be on the other, and I'd miss her.

So, you know, over the years—and it's really hard for me to admit this—I've actually, I swear this is true, taken steps to become a better person. Not tons of steps. Like I don't give handouts to junkies who knock on my door, and I still flip off the crack addict who pretends to collect donations for the deaf at the intersection near my house, and I'm still completely open to the idea of copious premarital sex, but I've willingly gone to church a few times over the past few years—seriously, I did—though I had to discontinue that when my favorite pastor left to open a coffeehouse in Decatur named The Gathering Grounds.

I thought about going with Kim to hers, but she lives eight hours away, and I met her pastor when I attended a church play in which my niece played a part, and he looked like he would pronounce "God" with two syllables. Plus, the only Bible I own was given to me by

The Good Sister

Grant, who had inscribed across the front, in big letters outlined in red-and-yellow oil paint, "Nothin' Harder Than a Preacher's Dick"— and Kim's congregation doesn't look to be the kind to appreciate that kind of humor.

Kim herself, though, doesn't judge. When we were kids, I was the runt of the family, and she was bigger than me even though I was older than her. My other siblings treated me like a kid-shaped kick-ball, and Kim could have easily followed suit. Instead she kept to her-self and read, or played cards with her stuffed monkey, or interacted with her other imaginary acquaintances, which I'm sure were kinder than her siblings, including me. Usually after I'd sustained a losing battle of some kind, I'd drag my crying, scratched, and pummeled hide to sit outside Kim's bedroom. I'd listen to her talk to her stuffed animals, sweetly teaching them what our mother taught us, like how to double down on a 10 when the dealer is showing a 6, among other nuggets of wisdom.

These days I still think about the divide between good and bad that I thought separated us, and I've come a long way since sitting, defeated, outside my little sister's door just to hear her voice. For one, I realize I switched to her side not because I always thought I was a bad person and needed to change, but because she always thought I was a good person and never asked me to.

Personal Demons

My friend Doug left town before we even got to see if his second exorcism was effective.

"My first exorcism had failed miserably," he said, dejectedly stating that the demon was still in him. I looked closely at him as I always did when Doug talked about his demon. I tried to see the evil he insisted was inside, but Doug didn't seem any more evil to me than he did the day I met him over a decade earlier. In fact, if you were to ask me, I would say Doug was one of the most demon-free people I know.

Our demons are for us to decide, as all demons are personal; that I know. Doug has since moved to New York to make a difference in the world by teaching inner-city high-school kids. I was a little worried when I heard he decided to do this. I thought that inner-city New York high-school kids would tear him up and crap him out their collective assholes if given the chance, but I also felt that Doug was doing the right thing, because often the best way to wrestle with demons is to stop looking inward and start looking outward, which is what Doug decided to do.

"Every day is crazier than the last," he reports. "I had the cops in my classroom yesterday because one of the seventh-graders started a fire. This is like a trip to Mars!"

He sounded happy, though, or at least less dejected about the presence of his demon than he did before.

We all have our demons to deal with, and believe me, I'd be grateful for my personal demon's presence if I were Doug, because it would mean I wouldn't have to face those kids alone. For example, one kid often, repeatedly, and very loudly tells Doug to suck his dick. I would find that, at the very least, an unsettling element to have to face in my daily life, but these are words that for Doug lost their shock value a long time ago. If he responds at all, it's simply to gasp in mock horror and say, "Such language!" then continue with the daily ministrations of dealing with the demons around him rather than in him. I have to say I admire him for that, and I wouldn't be surprised if some of his students do, too.

Lord knows I could have used a teacher like Doug when I was in high school. If I did, maybe someone would have noticed when I dropped out. I remember we had just moved and were set to face yet another new school, when the administrators had bewilderingly trusted me with my own school file to hand to my first-period teacher to announce my arrival and commence my registration. But instead of going to the classroom and thereby commencing another period of painful adjustment, I simply walked straight to the parking lot, got in my '69 VW Bug, and drove to the beach. After that I was happily lost in a crack, since my teachers, who didn't know to expect me, could not apprise the administrators and subsequently my mother of my absences. It was an ideal situation, I thought, and one that lasted three months. I would probably still be on that beach to this day if not for Kim turning me in.

At the time I thought it was because she was jealous, as every day when I dropped her off at school she had to go to class while I could U-turn my way to the beach and wallow another day away. But Kim didn't hate school like me; in fact, she was almost the opposite of me in every way. Where I was brusque, she was sweet, and while I had the soul of a sea urchin, she had the soul of a saint. She would join chess clubs while I befriended pyros behind the library and made fun of chess-club joiners. In fact, I often made the difficult transition to new schools even worse for her than they had to be, as sometimes my spikey-souledness would direct itself at her in the hallways.

I bet I know the real reason Kim might have turned me in. High school is hell enough when you know everyone, let alone when you don't. When I think of those months I left my little sister to make her way through another new school by herself—as soft-hearted and therefore ill-equipped as she was to withstand the cruelty of her peers—while I lived like a sand hobo, it's about all I can do to keep from calling her to beg her forgiveness. We all have our demons to deal with, and for all of my negative, misanthropic crustiness, I was Kim's own personal demon. And she was grateful for my presence, because it meant she didn't have to face those kids alone.

The Windup Monkey

THE LAST TIME I WAS IN MUNICH, I REMEMBER thinking I had better ways of wasting my time besides going to a toy museum. In fact, I seriously think I would have had more fun pushing buttons up my nostrils, as Kim did when she was three. I remember it really well, how my father was dashing for the car keys, bellowing about how Kim had shoved a button up her nose and now we had to take her to the hospital to crack open her nasal cavity and dig it out. At that point my sister, who was brilliant even at three (other than the button shoving), convinced my father she was just kidding and hadn't shoved anything anywhere. Then three years later she had to get her head X-rayed on account of how she somehow used it to pound a hole in our living room wall (all I know is that it was hardly my fault at all), and I'm told that the doctor clipped the film on the light tray, peered closely at the outline of Kim's skull, and exclaimed softly, "She has a button all up in her head." After that Kim got to stay in the hospital for a few days, where they served her hot chocolate every time she asked for it. So I'm not kidding when I said I'd have more fun shoving buttons up my nostrils than visiting a toy museum in Munich.

The toy museum came up every time we flew to Munich, as inevitably there would be a crew member who had never been, and just as inevitably they would try to enlist me, the German-interpreter flight attendant, to come along and translate everything.

First, I have to say, I am a lousy translator. What I don't know, I make up. Once, way back before I could say no, I got shanghaied by the crew into attending a tour of a castle outside of Frankfurt, where I was to serve as the interpreter to the actual tour guide. At the end of the tour, I had my fellow crew members believing that German royalty of the Renaissance era fertilized their gardens by sticking their actual asses out their turret windows to crap on the flower beds below. But in my defense I'm almost positive the tour guide really said that.

The toy museum, though, I had avoided all this time and I didn't plan on deviating. The German word for toy, *spielzeug*, for example, translates literally to *play device*, which is a damn boring way to refer to something supposedly fun, if you ask me. I envisioned the museum with row after row of old windup play devices encased behind glass. All of them made from wood probably, with placards before them that my bad German would butcher into warped facsimiles of their real meaning. "It says here," I would probably have said, "that this was painted with authentic human earwax."

I bet not even one of those toys would be as fun as the mess of electrical stuff I used to get as a kid. I remember one in particular, a set of plug-in metal molds that came with tubes of colored goop made from nuclear, cancer-inducing polypropylene, probably. You would squirt the goop onto the molds, which were in the shape of flowers, and then heat it up. The metal plates got so hot we could have used them to cauterize freshly amputated limbs. So what if we burned our

The Good Sister

fingers—we had a lovely collection of little choke-hazard-shaped rubber flowers to show for it.

But Kim's favorite toy did not even need to be plugged in. In fact it was a windup monkey that never left her side, with the fake fur rubbed down to just a rough nubbiness, pretty much. When wound up, it did the same thing, again and again, as far as I could tell. But for some reason it did other things for my sister. Somehow it performed all kinds of wondrous feats and mischief. Once we discovered Kim in the bottom bunk, with her monkey next to her, hanging by its feet. "I caught him cheating at cards," she said. Another time we found her with her head festooned in fresh daisies, brought to her, she said, by the windup monkey. For me, though, the monkey never cheated at cards or picked flowers; it just did the same thing again and again.

So I have never gone to the toy museum in Munich. I don't see the appeal of play devices behind a locked partition, things that if you wound them up, would do the same thing over and over again. Maybe I was worried that I'd realize that I was hardly any different, that maybe I should be more like my little sister, who saw such wonder in simple things, and who would have loved that museum and the treasures it held. But I had routinely been coming to Munich for over a decade, and I knew what I liked to do. I liked to lock my door, for one, and rest my rough nubbiness until it was time to wind myself up again.

Filthy Heathens

I'M HERE IN ENGLAND TRYING TO GET EXCITED about it being my last time, seeing as how my job for the airlines has taken a total toilet spin. It was a great job while it lasted, too—kept me equipped with somewhat of a toehold in the world of reality. Or it did up until I should have known the ride was over and made my way to an emergency exit. But it's hard to let go of a safety net, even if that safety net is suffocating you.

So here it is, my last time, and the only feeling I have is the vague sense that I'll miss those British prawn-flavored potato chips. That's it. I keep looking around, expecting to be overcome with melancholy, staving myself in case I'm suddenly fraught with despair over a future without kidney pie and spotted dick (whatever that is), waiting for it to hit me that this is the last time. But it doesn't.

This is a big change from my last last time in England. That was in the '80s when I was all young, permed, and oozing sentimentality like an untreated wound. I was a different person then, but England was different, too. It was a hell of a lot smellier, for one, and there were no automated teller machines that could suck money out of my American bank account—if I'd had one with money in it. Instead I had my mother's American Express card, which was supposed to be used for emergencies, and I remember calling her once to say I'd used it to buy beer during finals, and she'd said that sounded like an emergency to her.

I remember while I was at the bank to extract cash for that occasion, I somehow crossed paths with an elderly gentlewoman, who felt perfectly within her right to clout me on the head with her cane. It confused me so much I simply gawked back at her, certain it was an accident, but she raised her cane again and I had to tear out of there.

I still don't know what I did to raise her ire, but to this day it's a little disquieting to recall. People really don't expect handsome society ladies to walk into banks and start beating on people with their canes, so unless you're the one getting beat on, it goes fairly unnoticed. I could have called out for help, but I understood intrinsically that no one would believe me, so I just got out of the way. Besides, abuse is very embarrassing when you are the subject of it; that is why the truly abused—unless they hopefully learn otherwise—rarely speak up.

On the same street as the bank there was a disheveled old maniac who sat at her window every morning and shrieked the most creative insults at everyone who passed underneath. Her place was across from the bus stop, so her wrath was unavoidable. "Godless whore!" she screamed to me and my friends. It was a great way to start the day. I used to scream back at her until my friend Clay, another American, clapped his hand over my mouth one day and begged me not to disrespect her.

"Jesus God," I laughed at him. "She just called you a weak-kneed nutless wanker, and I can't talk back?"

But he pleaded with me. He explained that she was the aunt of his landlord, and how she suffered in the concentration camps of Austria during the Second World War, and now here she was with a weakened mind, left to scream verbal abuses from her balcony until the end of her days.

"Really?" I asked, getting choked up.

"No," he said. "But it could be."

I punched him. But still, after that I never yelled back at the lady. Clay's words had resonated with me, and I came to the further conclusion that people in pain, for whatever reason, often seek to intensify it by abusing others in hopes it will garner an agonizing retaliation.

"Godless heathen!" the lady shrieked from her window, and I could see it in her eyes, even from across the street, the rawness from whatever memories the cracks in her broken mind had uncovered. "Filthy godless heathen!" she screamed. No one responded. The crowd was thoroughly silent and awkward in the spew.

"That would be me," I finally said. "I'm the filthy godless heathen."

"No," said another, "I am."

"No, I'm the filthy godless heathen," laughed another, and soon there we all were, a bunch of filthy godless heathens laughing until the bus came and took us away.

By that time I'd been in Oxford for half a year, studying at a college that was separate from the actual famous university but that shared the same territory as well as a few of its professors just the same. One such professor was a local magistrate. I cannot for the life of me remember what she taught us. All I remember is that it would have helped my learning process if she'd have once bothered to put out her cigarette. I coughed as loud as a lawn mower during her tutorials.

By then my lungs were hardly more than two used teabags anyway, considering my parents smoked so much that over time streaks

The Good Sister

of nicotine would stain our ceiling like the splatter pattern at the scene of a slaughter.

I tell you, the British must be tough, because their collective secondhand cloud is so thick I'm surprised the whole country doesn't develop its own atmospheric ring like the planet Saturn or something. I was there barely a week before I got hit with a bout of bronchitis that nearly ripped the ribs right out of my chest. The doctor told me to stay out of the pubs, because that's where most of the smoke was. Stay out of the pubs? He may as well have told me to stop breathing— which, come to think of it, I almost did.

I stopped smoking myself when I was thirteen—one of the last times I ever acted with complete conviction. I remember that last cigarette perfectly. By then I'd been smoking four years and had—I swear to God—developed a pack-a-day habit. That night I sat on my friend's front steps inhaling this last cigarette like it could save my life, rather than prematurely snuff it out.

In fact, it seems that all my past last times were better than these recent ones. Here I am in England, with a fist full of prawn-flavored potato chips, trying to appreciate it being my last time here, wondering when I'll get all awash in sentiment and start worrying about losing my job along with my toehold in the world of reality, when all of a sudden I remember what Grant told me.

"Hollis, you don't live in the world of reality anyway," he said. "You live in the world of *possibility*."

He's right, I guess, so what the hell—why not make this the last time I think in terms of last times?

Boobs and Wiener

KIM'S HUSBAND, EDDIE, THE LAND BARON, is under siege by two crusty drug addicts who aren't even his tenants, which I find alarming given the contingent of dubious suspects who do actually occupy his rental properties. Granted, though, most of them are only trouble if they don't take their medication.

Take Octavia, who moved in last April and respectfully paid her rent on time for the first month, then promptly refused to fork over another penny seeing as how, she claimed, the house was filled with poisonous gas and all, which really put her out health-wise, so the very least she could expect in return was rent-free living for, like, ever. And by the way, she was happy to do him the favor of destroying the interior, too, by leaving the carpet looking and smelling like it was used to transport rotting corpses to their shallow graves.

It turns out Octavia wasn't very regimented with her medication. Now, thankfully, she is gone. It took four months, a marshal, and a magistrate (who scoffed at Eddie's late fees) to close the book on that fiasco. But the drama doesn't end there. At another property, Eddie has two other tenants he's in the process of evicting—a lesbian couple whose ex-husbands live down the street from them in another house. The one girl is a Denny's waitress and fairly bearable, while the other is a sluggish, drug-addled walrus who parties with the exes while her girlfriend is at work.

You'd think Eddie wouldn't involve himself, but Eddie always involves himself. He's a big walking bundle of open arms, I tell you,

The Good Sister

and I'd worry about him if I hadn't personally seen him get dragged behind a ton of horses and come up smiling. Seriously, the beatings, kicks, and scars—both emotional and physical—he's absorbed in his life would have hardened others into a small ball of bitterness, but Eddie always emerges bigger of heart and more open of arms. I marvel at him. I really do. I figure he makes a good role model, which is why I want to buy an investment property, too, while my credit report still says I'm employed. Eddie agreed and offered to show me the ropes.

Right now he is currently confronting the ex-husbands of his errant tenants, trying to run their petty drug-dealing asses out of the neighborhood. These two guys are known, believe it or not, as "Boobs" and "Wiener," the former nicknamed for his shirtless sagging man-tits, and the latter for his simple mental disposition. You might believe that two miscreants who go by Boobs and Wiener wouldn't pose such a threat, but they do. For example, since it's now established that the lesbian couple is moving, Eddie is showing the property to other possible tenants, which at first he had to do while Boobs and Wiener hung around out front, spitting on anyone ambling up the walk.

Now, after an encounter that afforded Eddie an opportunity to brandish his industrial stun gun and chase them through the neighborhood, they stay on their porch a few yards away and simply scream from there. This does not seem to bother Eddie in the least. Me? If I faced this, I'd want to tunnel my way underground to get away from them. Those two terrify me simply for what they represent, which is constant confrontation, and I hate confrontation. It produces an anxiety in me that is so severe I actually, on occasion, foam at the mouth. That's about the closest I can do to feigning an epileptic attack, which is how I've seen Lary successfully deflect oncoming panhandlers.

In fact, I have had people lie to me, all big-eyed and earnest, right to my face ("I swear, the panties in the glove compartment belong to my mother"), and normally I'm so mortified for them that I'll blather forth all kinds of opportunities for them to save themselves rather than witness their shame at being busted. I hate that about myself. I wish I could be more like Kim, who has a gaze as level as a laser and who is impervious to the squirming of those who have been confronted with their own idiocy.

I have been on the other end of that gaze. "I swear," I told her when I was a drug-addled college student and we were roommates on campus, "he was just sleeping there in bed with me, that's all. Nothing happened. He has a girlfriend, for chrissakes." Kim did not have to say a word; she just leveled her look on me and kept it there. I squirmed like a caterpillar under a pin but never came clean. Still, though, I remember how it felt to be confronted with my own idiocy, thank God, because by now I've learned that if we're not strong enough to confront the idiocy in others, we're less likely to face it in ourselves.

So Boobs and Wiener continue to scream at Eddie, but at least they do it from their own porch now, as opposed to the sidewalk in front of Eddie's property. Kept at that distance, those two do seem a lot less sinister, powerless even, seeing as how their only power lies in their ability to put people at unease. Boobs braves a few steps forward, but Eddie keeps him at bay with a simple wave of his stun gun, an effective reminder that he, for one, is not afraid of confrontation.

The Good Sister

Among the Rubbish

I DID NOT SET OUT YESTERDAY TO SOLVE A BANK HEIST. Nope. When I woke up in the morning, my only plan was to buy an investment property as Eddie advised, because it's not like I can rely on my 401K for retirement—a 401K that is empty now, actually, but no big deal.

So I want to invest in something other than stocks, and something more reliable than, for example, the savings plan of my friend Wes, who years ago figured he'd found a rare penny and could retire on its proceeds once he alerted Sotheby's of his discovery. The last time I saw Wes, he was literally shirtless and barefoot, conducting a yard sale from his girlfriend's driveway. Not that I have anything against that. My own mother took to hawking boxes of picked-over discards at a swap meet once her job building bombs for the government finally fell apart. She made ends meet by selling crap out of the back of an old VW van. She wore a coin belt and everything. I'd never seen her so happy. Eventually she got good at recognizing the occasional gem among the rubbish, such as the Italian Pezzato figurine she gave me. She found it in a box of broken coffee saucers, a perfect little jewel discovered among the rubbish.

Which aptly describes my real-estate investment technique: Either find the gem among the rubbish or find the rubbish among the gems. Lately my method has been to search out the ugliest house on the block, and yesterday I had one all picked out—a tiny brick shit box that sat like a little boil in a neighborhood of ostentatious new-builts, and if there's anything I can't resist, it's an ugly house sitting squat among its pastel-painted neighbors. The house I live in now is like that, barely bigger than the trailers that sit in our driveway, with aluminum grandma awnings and a bathroom smaller than my bed. I'd initially bought it as my first rental property until the crotchety neighbor next door stalker-called me twenty times one day to bitch about the "bad element" that renters bring and how I needed to live there myself in order to keep the neighborhood from going "completely to the pooper."

"All right," I finally sighed, as I'm a pushover for senile old porcupines. So I moved in and Dot and I talk across the fence fairly often now. She forgets she already told me the story about how the lady who lived here before me died of breast cancer twenty years ago at the age of forty-two, so she recounts it to me again and again, and I always listen to her patiently, pretty much. Some mornings I still catch her in her bath slippers in the street trying to pick up industrial trace material that had fallen off the contractor trucks headed to the new development down the street. Today our houses are among the last holdouts in a now-hot neighborhood—the few that are not torn down and not improved.

So this brick shit shack I had picked out met all this same criteria. It was a veritable shoo-in until, for some reason, I was drawn to another house entirely. It was not the ugliest house on the block, but rather one of the better scraps among the rubbish; a potentially cute but ancient shotgun shack with hardly any black-widow spiders in the meter well or used condoms in the yard or any of the other things I usually regard as good-luck tokens. I pretty much appreciate anything

The Good Sister

that will scare off other buyers and allow the house to sit there and so confound the seller that they'll piss with happiness at the sound of my offer. The first house I ever bought stood a few doors down from where the police had recently found a severed human head in a plastic sack. So you can imagine the bargains to be had on that street. But this house had none of that and it still spoke to me, which made me suspicious.

"There's nothing wrong with this place," I said apprehensively to Ramiro, my long-suffering real-estate agent, "so what's wrong with this place?"

"If you don't buy it," he sighed as he peered at the slice of skyline view through the living-room wraparound windows, "I will."

"Let's check out the basement," I ventured cautiously. So Ramiro opened the hatch and there it was! Right there on the dirt floor was a stolen ATM machine! How awesome is that? The house was passable in every aspect except it happened to be a crime scene involving a nearby bank robbery! This beats a severed head in a plastic sack by miles! Soon the place was surrounded by police cars and Ramiro was busy recounting his statement to a gaggle of officers with their pens poised. "I'm sorry, Hollis," he hollered to me amid the frenzy. "I apologize for getting you into this."

I answered him but he didn't hear me over the helicopter blades rotating overhead.

"I said," I shouted, barely able to contain my excitement, "that I'll take it!"

The Man Who Died Twice

I'VE DECIDED TO MURDER A MAN NAMED TRAVIS. I hope he doesn't take it personally. I don't even know him. It's his friends I hate. They call me at all hours, with their unlisted phone numbers, asking if he's around. At first I was polite. "Sorry, wrong number," I'd chirp. But then after the fiftieth call, I decided Travis had to die.

"You haven't heard?" I gasped. "Travis, poor thing, was anally raped by his prison inmates with a cafeteria table leg. He died the next day."

Travis doesn't always die the same way, and sometimes he doesn't die at all, but horrible things happen to him, over and over again. "I'm sorry to be the first to tell you, but Travis died horribly in a grease fire." Sometimes Travis is not all the way dead yet. "You should go visit him in the hospital," I might advise. "Maybe he'll recognize you. The doctor said the late-stage syphilis has only eaten half his brain."

His friends might show some polite concern, until the lurid details emerge; then they hang up. I've decided Travis must be a crystal-meth dealer, because why else would his pussy friends all have unlisted numbers, and why else would they call him at all hours? "They say if he lives," I console, "he'll have to wear a diaper and carry a doughnut cushion for the rest of his life."

I've had this cell number for like a hundred years, so it's not that I innocently inherited the old number of this Travis guy. No, this Travis guy plucked my number out of the air and is giving it to people he hopes to avoid, obviously, which is another reason he merits a painful death.

The Good Sister

"He was killed by an infected, ulcerated hemorrhoid," I might elaborate. "It's not as uncommon as you might think. They've created a memorial fund. For more information, go to www.travistheasstard.com."

I started to feel bad when one girl burst into tears upon hearing the news. Of course, she could have been crying because her drug supply just dried up, but at that point I realized that prick Travis was blowing people off who actually gave a crap about him. "Don't feel bad," I consoled her. "The police found a huge cache of kiddie porn in his lean-to, so he deserved to die."

I got busted when one guy called back and got a second rendition of Travis' death. "A man can't die twice," he hollered. Immediately I employed one of my best methods of defense, which was to imperson-ate my eighty-five-year-old neighbor, Dot, who has Alzheimer's. This impersonation entails a lot of screaming. "I said I want my milk with my meal!" I bellowed again and again. It's a very effective ploy, and works against telemarketers, too.

The only problem is that the ruckus sometimes summons Dot to my door. She is a good neighbor, and when she hears screaming, dammit, she's gonna investigate. I wish I could say the same for when I hear screaming from her place, but the truth is I hear it so often it's just part of the background noise now. I like Dot, though. On her good days we joke about how we're gonna go get us some men. "I see some across the street right now," she'll cackle, pointing at the shirtless contractors working on a house that, until now, had been one of the few on our street that had accompanied ours among the unrenovated. "You go get 'em," she urges. "I'm too tired."

This wasn't one of Dot's good days, though. "My husband's dead," she sobbed, her eyes wild and searching. I nodded sympathetically. Dot's husband died more than twenty years ago. "I don't understand. I buried him twenty-five years ago, but I woke up this morning and he was dead all over again."

I invited her to come inside, sit on my new patio, and have a cup of tea, but she declined. "I have so many things to do," she worried. "That man was the love of my life. How could he leave me like that? He did it to himself, you know. He used to call me from his office every day, but that day he didn't call me, and I knew something was wrong. That's where they found him, in his office. He did it to himself. What will people say? I don't want people talking."

"Screw what people say, Dot," I said, walking her back to her porch. "That should be the last thing on your list of concerns."

"He was the love of my life," she sighed, "and I thought I was his. So many things to do, and I already did it all once. I woke up this morning and he was dead all over again," she repeated, her eyes pleading. "I didn't know a man could die twice."

Sometimes I wonder if crazy people are crazy because they're mercilessly attuned to everything, even thoughtless phone conversations a whole house away. In any case, that morning I got a glimpse of the inner prison where Dot must live. Her husband's death was the most painful thing she ever endured. She took a decade to get over it, only to succumb to Alzheimer's and forget she got over it. I stayed there a good while that morning, holding an old woman's hand, helping her live through the fresh agony of losing her husband, the man who had died twice.

The Good Sister

Beaten and Scarred

MY BROTHER-IN-LAW EDDIE COULDN'T POSSIBLY be mistaken for a gay man, ever, not even if there was a dick in his mouth at the time. For example, he's been here in Atlanta for five days now, suffering a hellacious cold, and he refuses to let me bother to buy him tissues, preferring instead to scrape his face with paper towels. "I don't need that tissue shit," he explains. "My nose is made of rhino hide."

So you'll understand why I laughed like a stoner when he expressed his concerns about being mistaken for a flamer when we borrowed Grant's truck yesterday. Grant's truck, "Fish Stick," is a rusty orange road hazard with a marionette trophy for a hood ornament, batons in the gun rack, and a license plate that reads GAY 269. Even so, when Eddie expressed his concern, I had to stop and catch my breath, bent over at the waist and everything, because I haven't had such a yuck in months. "Eddie," I finally wheezed, "the only way someone could confuse you with a gay man is if they'd been blind since birth."

Eddie was born in South Africa to Swiss parents and had a childhood of the kind that affords him such fond memories as the time his mother got pissed on by a puma. He looks (and dresses) like Crocodile Dundee, talks with the accent of a British expatriate, and speaks several obscure languages of both "bush" and European varieties. He has camped in the Serengeti, communed with elephant herds, and killed cobras. Even today, here in Atlanta, he never carries fewer than three knives at a time, one hardly smaller than a machete, and damn if they don't reliably prove to be useful somehow or another. "Let me get that for you," he recently told a hardware store associate who had trouble releasing the spout on a five-gallon bucket of anti-mildew treatment. Out came Eddie's "small" knife, and in seconds he had that thing deftly hacked open like a hyena carcass. Now that's a handy talent.

I wasn't always so appreciative.

Years ago Eddie met Kim in Zurich and claimed her with a fierce, cavemanlike determination. At the time, my mother hated him and I did my best to do the same, though unlike my mother I was fortunate enough to outlive my own orneriness.

In Zurich, Eddie fit in like a gorilla at a wedding reception; a walking wad of Y chromosomes in dingo boots and tooled leather among a society of indifferent pussies living rich off a national commitment to staying uninvolved in anything but currency. When I met him, all I saw was a big drunk scarred from too many bar fights and bush wranglings. When Kim met Eddie, though, she saw something much different. In fact, maybe when he claimed her like an alpha male in a pride of lions, it was not out of determination but desperation, as lifelines are funny things, often coming unexpectedly to those whose lives they are saving. Eddie married Kim five years later and, having been redeemed himself, now makes a living redeeming others by counseling the drug-afflicted in Dayton.

But here he is in Atlanta, scraping and hammering and basically building a home where there hardly was one before. All of this because it turns out I am the reluctant owner of a slum that has been sucking the life out of my eye sockets lately. The tenants moved out with no notice after somehow transforming my formerly passable rental

The Good Sister

property into a roach-infested shotgun shack with moldy walls, rotted flooring, and carpet that looked like it was recovered from the dump after someone used it to wrap roadkill scraped up from the freeway. Looking at the house made me want to simply fall over backward and bawl, as all I saw was something beaten and scarred beyond redemption. It all seemed so insurmountable, and my mounting debt made me feel like I'd just been crapped through the ass of life. *If I were a house,* I thought when I saw it, *this would be me.*

But Eddie saw something different. Of course, all my local friends are far too fed up with me, or just too generally useless, to help me renovate a whole house (Keiger, for one, showed up in a tangerine-colored cashmere sweater, gingerly sipping a cup of artisan coffee). So I could be trapped into thinking it's fairly pathetic I had to import a family member from Dayton to help me out, but I know I'm actually lucky. From the start Eddie was unfazed. "Piece of cake," he said, looking around at the roach droppings and rot, scraping his nose with a paper towel. "This is nothing," he smiled, prying open a pail of plaster with his knife. And with that, Eddie, no longer beaten and scarred, set about redeeming the unredeemable.

The Sell Out Center

UNLIKE THE USUAL GAGGLE OF PUSSIES who comprise my close friends—all of whom scattered like fruit bats at the first sign I might need help fixing my new slum—I also have friends who are actual contractors. Take the very reliable Art, for example. If I need something done to a house, I usually call him and he is very reliable about coming over and telling me what is necessary for me to do it correctly. Then I'll inform him that I have, maybe, five dollars set aside to accomplish it all, at which point he very reliably falls over in a fit of gibbering laughter, pats me on the back, and wishes me luck.

Thus, armed with the knowledge Art has imparted, I'll invariably set about slopping together a big, splinter-ridden Band-Aid of an attempt to follow his instructions, which in this case entailed the enlistment of my brother-in-law Eddie to come here and hammer on my rental house until it sort-of-kinda-quasi resembled, if you drank a six-pack and squinted your eyes, a house again.

Take the kitchen counter. The former tenants must have used it to perform alien autopsies or something, because I have never seen anything so destroyed. It was cheap to begin with, just compressed sawdust cemented between two thin layers of laminate the color of dental cavities. Then somehow moisture had seeped under the encasement—and it must have been a lot of moisture over a long period of time—because all around the edges the counter was bloated, cracked, and crumbling.

The Good Sister

"This will have to go," Art said, tapping the counter, creating a small cloud of escaping mildew. "No shortcuts here, Hollis," he eyed me gravely. "I mean it."

His concern is warranted because he's helped me renovate my own home over the course of our seven-year friendship, and I estimate probably half the work he's done was dedicated solely to the undoing of various corners I've attempted to cut here and there, such as the time I figured foundation concrete would make a perfectly fine floor for my in-home office. So Art knew I was eyeing that counter as a beast to be circumvented, wondering if it couldn't be fixed with some superglue or a stapler. Looking back, I must say I'm a little touched by his unrelenting crusade to make an honorable home restorer out of me.

But I am who I am. Art finished emphasizing the importance of accuracy in calculating the various corners of the counter, and how they'd need to be either cut professionally by a gemologist (practically) or come factory-cut in sections sold at Home Depot—both of which were options that would ensure the counter cost me more than its weight in cocaine. Afterward I hopped in my car with Eddie and proceeded straight to the Sell Out Center.

First, I love the name of this place, as I never fail to find it apt as I approach it from across the parking lot, which is itself the size of a sovereign country but still not big enough to dwarf the gargantuan, seven-billboards-big sign announcing the Sell Out Center, which features the Mount Rushmore face of a '50s housewife who is apparently orgasmic over the galaxy of salvaged furniture and appliances inside.

The inventory consists of anything that could be moved or pried loose from liquidated hotels, restaurants, industrial factories, disputed territories, religious compounds, Iraqi palaces, and any other place that up and shut down suddenly under a shower of unrest, financial or otherwise. The couches are the kind you find in bank lobbies, each weighing as if they'd been stuffed with two or three concrete-encased mafia hit victims. Massive fixtures, mascots, and signage hang from the ceiling on hooks like it was a butcher shop for dismembered Mardi Gras floats. Dusty, glassed-in shelves throughout the place showcase a gritty little population of kitschy oddities, which further gives the place a great, science-fair feel, like any second you'll discover the fetus of a two-faced kitten in a jar of formaldehyde.

I have never once bought anything there, and this day was no different, as everything they offer is so huge, and my need is never large enough to fit the inventory. Today, it turned out all the store had that could pass for a kitchen counter looked as though it came from the cafeteria of an old prison, and not even Eddie could have hammered *that* into shape. But still, I'll use any excuse to go back there. There is just something about the place, the piled-up pieces of other people's worlds; the fifty identical armchairs, half with ripped upholstery; the rolls of putty-colored carpet as big as redwood trunks; the wardrobe mirrors stacked twenty deep, some broken, possibly having already unleashed an eternity of cursed fortune. It literally looks like a hundred little planets came crashing to a stop in that very spot. I don't think it hurts to become comfortable in a place like that, as you never know when it might be your world that will end up here because, like mine, the company you work for went bankrupt. If it does, then that's all right. Let people pick it over. Let them climb the giant carcasses of your past. You are still who you are. You do what you need to do, day by day. You smile or you don't. You sell out or you don't.

A Fascinating Specimen

MY FLOOR BUFFER AND I ARE IN BATTLE. Well, it's not exactly *my* floor buffer. I rented it from Home Depot during a moment of characteristic indecisiveness.

"Are you completely refinishing your floors or just polishing them?" the associate asked.

Lord, what does he mean by completely refinish? I hate to do anything *completely.* The wood floors at my rental house are sixty-eight years old, and my real-estate agent Ramiro told me that if I wanted to sell the place, I'd need to pull up the carpet and refinish the floors. But once you pull up carpet, you're sorta committed to what's underneath, and I'm not ready to commit to that—and I'm also not all that committed to selling it, either—so I decided to just pull up the carpet in the living room to see how it looked in that patch alone.

It did not look good. But what do I know about how sixty-eight-year-old wood floors are supposed to look when they've been covered with rotting carpet for decades? I keep thinking of the Ice Man mummy they pulled out of a glacier over a decade ago that caused such a stir. "Wonderfully preserved," everybody said, when to me it looked like he'd been crapped out the ass of a diseased mastodon. Still the mummy sparked a field day of speculation on how he might have died. Did he die in battle? Was he felled by the arrow of a rival warrior? Whatever happened, it's believed he escaped the battle and died at a distance after arranging his equipment next to him in a neat pile.

The Good Sister

"A fascinating specimen," scientists blathered, thrilled because they had their own criteria and the mummy met it.

I was hoping maybe home buyers were like that, too. I know most want everything to be shiny and new and smelling of putty, and there are others that love things to be "wonderfully preserved." My friend once bought a house where the hardwood floors had been used as a collective toilet by all the neighborhood crack whores, yet he bought it because it still had half a historical fireplace mantel that remained "wonderfully preserved."

"I think I'm just going to polish the floor," I told the Home Depot associate, who then explained the different grades of buffer pads I had to choose from. Evidently there are as many kinds of buffer pads as there are particles of silt that had matriculated through my old carpet and then fused with foot sweat and spilled beer to create the dried paste that now needed to be scraped up from the floorboards. So I simply picked the pad that was the most sandpapery of textures without its being actual sandpaper. Because if it were actually sand-paper, then I would be completely refinishing the floors, and I'm not ready to commit to that.

"Make sure you have the handle locked and you brace it against your leg before you turn it on," the Home Depot guy said, showing me the little switch.

A floor buffer looks like one of those metal detectors that geri-atrics use when they hunt for lost watches on the beach, only the buffer is enormous and quite likely made from melted communist statues. And it spins. To get that thing to my property, I practically had to hook it to my bumper and tow it there. Once inside the house I plugged it in and flipped the switch. The only thing is I forgot to lock the handle and brace it against my leg like the Home Depot guy advised me, and all I have to say is this: If a Home Depot guy ever uses the words "lock and brace" regarding a piece of equipment, I suggest you take that very seriously.

The amount of destruction that buffer did with the simple flipping of a switch was awe-inspiring. The buffer drum spun with the speed of a boat propeller, causing the whole contraption to spring from my fingers and hit the wall with the velocity of an airplane crash. I tried again a number of times, but no amount of bracing and locking could control it. Unfailingly, when I flipped the switch, the buffer would fly out of my hands and then around the room, crashing into things, including me; it was akin to getting hit by a wrecking ball. In the end, the buffer did nothing but beat the hell out of me and everything else in the room. Finally I simply decided to escape the battle and crawl, bleeding, to a distant corner. There I lay quietly, my equipment next to me. Maybe the discovery of my remains will cause a stir, I thought. Maybe I will be considered a fascinating specimen.

Rented Men

GRANT KEEPS SAYING I HAVE LESBIAN TASTE. He feels that just because I buy crap from IKEA and drive a PT Cruiser—in other words, just because I have a sense of practicality—I am automatically a repressed lesbian and I should just drop the hetero act and situate my strap-ons right now.

"It's the truth," he insists, taking another sip from his pussy-ass iced Americano probably made from coffee beans plucked from leopard turds off the floor of the rain forest.

"Look who's talking," I tell him. "You've only been gay for maybe 20 percent of your entire life at the most. Don't talk to me about the truth, because the truth is you don't know shit."

But the real truth is I don't think Grant is really gay; I just think he's really horny and other men are the only creatures on the earth who can match his appetites. My theory is he kept it all in check for the first forty or so years of his life so he could father a child with his first ex-wife, who mysteriously doesn't speak to him anymore. I personally think she should foam at the mouth and fall all over herself in gratitude for the fact that Grant stayed straight long enough to father their wonderful kid, but I am incredibly biased seeing as how I love Grant madly. But not the father-my-child kind of love or even the satisfy-your-appetites-on-me kind of love, but the you're-a-stupid-puckered-poohole kinda love, which is the best kind.

Now that we got that out of the way, it was time to get down to the real reason I was there watching Grant gingerly slurp at his artisan coffee elixir, and that is because I need him to help me pick up Mexicans. Because if anybody is an expert at picking up Mexicans, it's Grant. Back when he had his Honda Element, otherwise known (by me) as the Bionic Anal-Sex Vessel, he would troll Buford Highway almost every night and pick up prospects like plucking berries from a bush. He would never go into explicit details with me because there is still that odd sort of gentleman side to him that is so maddening, but to this day he prefers Mexicans over any other kind of 'cans. He eats them up like popcorn shrimp.

My own appetites are embarrassingly pedestrian by comparison. I don't need men in my life right now for anything except painting my duplex. Hopefully a new tenant will be moving in any day, and even though Eddie has scraped and chiseled the place into a passable habitat, it still looks worse than that Iraqi shit pit they pulled Saddam out of. It needs paint, putty, plaster, caulk, and a total HAZMAT hose-down. I've been working on it so hard this past week that my hands look like I clawed my way out of a coffin.

My guy friends are all pretty useless in this regard. For example, Keiger came over the other day to say hi, and while he was here, I asked him to help me position something. Okay, it was a rusty burglar bar, and okay, it was pretty heavy, but you would have thought I'd asked him to build me a bomb shelter. He spent the entire rest of the visit brushing off his Bermuda shorts like an obsessive-compulsive coming off medication.

I can't deal with that. I'd rather just rent men. I hear it's a fairly easy process. You just go to the hardware-store parking lot where they hang out in the early morning, hoping to be chosen. The only problem is I thought I should have a guy with me to do the brokering, and I thought Grant should be the guy because I've already way overtaxed my relationship with Lary. The last time I went to Lary's, just to borrow his jigsaw and get a ten-hour tutorial on how to cut countertops, he took his shotgun out and started to reassemble it. This is his secret signal to let me know he needs me to get the fuck out of his house. But I had to go alone to rent the men because after Grant's bartending gig at The Local, a detonating grenade wouldn't wake him up.

Alone at the Men-Rental Depot, my selection process entailed picking the man with the kindest face and then asking him to choose his own workmate. I then took them to the duplex, told them what to do, and they set about doing it.

When I came back in four hours, it was done. It was that simple. I didn't have to beg, wheedle, bawl, promise marathon blowjobs, or anything. All I did was pay them and when the work was done, they went away. The best part is I didn't have to hear about how five years ago they once loosened a lug nut for me and how that right there is reason enough to forever harangue me for being a burdensome, ovary-bearing albatross in their lives. This "pay/go away" process is much better. It's like I discovered a whole new world.

"Lesbian," Grant taunts me.

"Whatever," I say. "Call me Rosie."

The Odd Pod Person

EDDIE RETURNED TO OHIO SOME TIME AGO. I suppose it had to happen sooner or later. But too bad he couldn't stick around for when it came time to rent my newly spackled slum, because I was surprised at how much I hated that process; having to break up my day to drive there and endure the presence of people who don't have the heart to tell you no, so they tell you anything else instead. "It's great." "I love it." "I'll take it." Translation: "I just wanna get to my car, and you're standing in my way."

I have absolutely no endurance for that, and I can't enlist my regular friends because they are impervious to my plight. For one, Grant is always absent whenever actual elbow grease is in order; he simply lifts like a fog. Lary and Daniel are more receptive to being plied for plebe duty, but, like Grant, they are two of my old friends, which means I've tapped that vein so many times it won't even rise anymore. I thought about extorting help from Keiger, but he's immune to my wiles these days. Last time he took me on a date he ditched me at a movie theater, and not even on purpose. He just got up to use the restroom or something and I slipped his mind.

So after one week I was ready to pussy out and stop posting it all together, figuring it would just fill up on its own, word of mouth or whatever, but then I saw a big crowd at Grant's door because he'd put his modern life on sale on eBay again. Every so often Grant puts all his modern furniture up for auction—flawless Saarinen tables, Herman Miller chairs, atomic-age pottery, and what all, fabulous stuff—but nothing people can't find within an hour of their own home if they looked hard enough. But still Grant had people like this couple yesterday, who flew in from Indiana to pick up some bookshelves they could have bought blocks from their own home, probably. But they were there less for the shelves than for the gravitational pull of Grant's sonic energy. His ad on eBay alone is a masterpiece of humor and mirth, promising all kinds of cosmic vibe to go along with his collection. It's all perfectly in keeping with Grant's philosophy: Energy attracts energy.

So I figured what worked for him would work for me. "Great house plus naked girls!" my rental postings blared. "Comes with free margaritas!" "Keg parties okay!" "(That part about naked girls is subject to change at any time.)" Because I'm tired of placing sanitary descriptions of my place only to get e-mails from "Tiffany," who is transferring here from Kansas City, and would like to know if I can pick her and her mother up at the airport to take her on a personal tour. And I'm tired of making appointments to show the place to prospective renters only to stand on the stoop and watch them turn back when they see the pile of tires on the corner. They're just tires, people! And not only that, but they've been painted pink and made into planters; for chrissakes, have you no appreciation for art?

So I'm honest with people. It's best for everyone. That way I don't have to waste half my day conducting needless junkets to my in-town rental house only to meet dazed, displaced suburbanites who embarrass us both by, as in the case of one single dad, pretending to like the place only to insist that it's his kid who has all the reservations. "I love it and I'd move here in a minute," the guy said, "but little Apple here thinks it's too far from the wine bar."

So no "sunny, charming in-town bungalow" platitudes in my postings anymore, because evidently that translates into way too many possibilities for people. That kind of talk is a complete blank slate, evidently, as people actually show up expecting to see a vacation cottage complete with serene meadow when it says right there, right next to their damn eyeballs, that the house is six minutes from downtown. Down-goddamn-town, so don't flip like a flapjack the second you hear a helicopter overhead. It's probably not a SWAT team; it's probably just surveillance, which is, you know, a good thing. Probably.

They could probably use more helicopters in suburban Ridge Springs or Spring Ridge or wherever the goddamn hell it is that apron-wearing housewives are cooking up their crystal meth these days. At least in the city you know what you're getting. I remember I lived in the suburbs for nine regrettable months once, where I fit in like a hobo at Sunday brunch. My neighbors practically converged with torches to run me out of there.

It's not like I didn't try to fit in, either. I even play tennis, for chrissakes. In fact, I'm freakishly good at tennis, as I was born with a natural talent for thwacking the crap out of balls. So I joined my subdivision's tennis team. They had to let me in because they had no choice, as it's unlawful to discriminate. There was no set roster, just an informal network of games based on invitations from other subdivisions. After a few games where I showed up in cutoffs and beheaded a few opponents with line drives at the net, I stopped getting invited to play. "What's the matter with you pussies?" I complained to my "teammates" at the poolside mixers. They all just gingerly plated their finger foods and turned away. See, that's how they get around the appearance of discrimination: They let you join, they just don't let you play.

So I figured it simply did not make business sense to post ads with pasteurized wording that attracted any more slumming suburbanites to the property just to have them sniff disapprovingly at the weathered exterior and the pile of rusty discarded appliances down the street. *Lord,* I thought. *That's nothing. C'mon, people.* "This is not a suburban cul-de-sac," I posted. "Ineffectual yuppy suck-ups please don't respond." "NO POD PEOPLE!"

But I think I overdid it, because Lord did that last part piss off some people. Who would have thought it was possible to offend pod people? I mean, I thought that was the main benefit of being a big vapid bucket of nothingness, because what better way to avoid hurt feelings than by having no feelings at all? And besides, when I blared "NO POD PEOPLE" in the heading of my Craigslist posting, I wasn't announcing my desire to exclude a particular group from responding to my ad for a house for rent; I was actually touting the neighborhood the house was in. It's a "cool, integrated neighborhood," I yodeled, "with lots of young artist types. The *opposite* of yuppie jog-stroller hell misery. The *opposite* of a pasteurized latte-sucking flavorless black-hole neighborhood populated by pod people."

See? No pod people, as in yippee, there's no pod people. Not no pod people, as in pod people need not apply. But then some asstard e-mailed me promising to flag my ad as discriminatory, thereby making me answerable to the fair-housing law, and if I don't clean up, I'll be liable for blahbity blahbity fucking blah.

Well, pod people, come and get me then. I'd be happy to let one of those cow-eyed pod suburbotrons rent my house if they wanted to. Seriously, have at it. Who's to say whether the total absence of pod people might be a quality that actually appeals to the odd pod person? At least they'll stand out from the crowd, and if their neighbors don't like them, they'll look them right in the eye and say so. There's something to be said about that. They won't ask them to join a damn club and then turn their back on them. They won't include you to exclude you. It might do the odd pod person good to break free of the frozen pond and come on over to where neighbors open their front doors and let their roiling underbellies right on out into the daylight. They can teach us how to appear not to discriminate, and we'll teach them how to make a pink planter out of an abandoned tire. There you have it: perfect harmony—for nine months, tops, before the villagers start to gather their torches.

The Good Sister

Burning Down the House

LARY IS AT A LOSS AS TO WHY I'D TURN DOWN his offer to burn down my house. He thinks it would be the answer to all my problems. "And this is the perfect season for arson, too," he insists. "Homeless people all over the place are lighting fires to keep warm; no one would even question it. You can blame it on a crackhead. A *homeless* crackhead. They're great scapegoats. How could you pass this up?"

"You worthless sack of maggots," I fume. "I cannot burn down my house and blame it on a crackhead."

First, I finally found a decent tenant to live in the house Lary wants to torch. Second, thanks to Eddie, it's not even the house itself that is giving me problems, but the water pipe in front of the house, somewhere under the sidewalk, that is busted. My water bill last month was almost as much as my mortgage. I called the city water department to report the leak, but the woman on the other end said the leak was on my property, which I doubted because, unless I own the sidewalk, I don't see how it could be on my property.

So I called back first thing the next morning and got another water-department lady who told me it said right there on her computer screen that I was told there was a leak on my property. I took issue with that, too, because of all the people telling anyone anything, I was the only one who actually laid personal eyes on the leak, with my property way over there, and the leak way over here, and again, unless I own the sidewalk it was not on my property.

"I'm telling you," Lary keeps insisting, "just fling a few crack lighters around for the firemen to sift out afterward, and no one will question a thing."

Lary has been hoping I'd burn my houses down for years now, in one way or another, as he's feeling harried because he is usually the second one I call during the unrelenting storm of broken crap that is homeownership. Grant is usually the first, because Grant has numbers to call and a passel of reliable fabrications to claim, and before you know it the entire citywide infrastructure is lining up to take the blame and send trucks to make things right.

Also, he's usually pretty generous about imparting this wisdom to me. But I'm not talking to Grant these days because he banished me to the storage closet of his gallery during the holiday art tour at the loft complex where he lives. All I wanted to do was set up a little stand to display a few homemade potholders and possibly some finger paintings by my little girl. Lord Christ, what was so bad about that? But Grant said it was his show and even if he gave me a tiny space in his gallery, it would make everything be about me, and the one thing that pisses the crap out of me is when Grant

The Good Sister

109

accuses me of being self-involved just because I want to commandeer his special event.

So it's straight to Lary this time, because for all his felonious bloviating, Lary is really good at finding what is wrong and fixing it. The problem is that he fancies himself a creator, not a fixer, and he would rather burn the broken thing to the ground and build a whole new thing. A bigger, better thing with turrets and whirligigs, preferably. I used to be like that, too, but now I like to keep the things I have and simply fix them when they break. I never knew how to fix things before, but I've been watching Lary fix stuff for fifteen years and now I fancy myself somewhat handy. I even have a tool belt. We never covered leaky underground pipes, though.

"I'm not burning the house down," I tell him.

"Then call Grant," Lary suggests. "He was just saying yesterday how bad he felt for hurting your feelings."

I did call Grant, but he was damn discourteous for someone in the throes of regret. "Bitch, I see that you don't want to hear what I'm saying," he said. "I am not sorry." But I did hear what he was saying, I just disagreed with it. So we screamed at each other for a few minutes until things were better between us.

I still have a busted water pipe, but at least I also have these two beloved bottom-fish who are my friends, one who didn't get burned to the ground and replaced, and the other who is good at finding what is wrong and fixing it.

Water Issues

MY PLUMBER, BEAR, SAYS I HAVE WATER ISSUES. She says this while covered in mud she dug up from my front yard in order to access the broken pipe that is the reason my water bill was bigger than my car payment last month. She has the piece of pipe in her hand, with the little pinhole in it where the rust had finally corroded through after forty years.

"Major water issues," she reiterates.

"All that water leaked out of that tiny little pinhole?" I ask.

"That's all it takes," she says.

I would marry Bear if it didn't promise to be such a complicated union, the biggest obstacles being that she already has a wife and I'm not gay. So I'll have to thank her with actual payment for her services instead. But this is not the end of my water issues. Both of my other properties have sprung leaks as well. The house where I actually reside is the worst all of a sudden. For some reason, whenever I run the washing machine, the bathroom floor gets flooded.

"What the hell is happening?" I gripe.

"Issues," Bear says, shaking her head as she hands me my bill.

Milly says I have angered the water gods, but everything is an angered god to her these days because of the Japanese anime-inspired cartoon marathon she watched with her cousin over Thanksgiving. I don't think I have angered any gods any more than normally lately, but it does seem weird that these water issues have popped up at all my addresses all at once and all of a sudden.

The Good Sister

I'm starting to think it was easier when I didn't even have any address at all to call my own. When I was growing up, my parents always rented our houses, and if there was ever a water issue we would just move. We moved four times in one year once, and it's funny, but we always lived near water, come to think of it, on either the California or Florida coast. Now the closest ocean to me is four hours away. The last time I drove there, I heard Shirley MacLaine on NPR talking about her own leaky pipes, I swear this is true, and how she went to an Indian shaman and was told that, because she had been refusing to cry herself lately, her house had begun to cry for her.

"Jesus, what a bionic nutball," I said to myself, even though I love Shirley MacLaine and thought she kicked ass as Aurora in *Terms of Endearment.* In fact, I remember I saw that movie just as I was about to move abroad to study in Oxford, England. I watched it with my favorite boyfriend of all time, Jeff, who was a surfer and practically lived in the water. At the end of the movie, I turned to see that he'd been crying and I, like, *laughed,* because this was Jeff, and Jeff didn't *cry.*

"Pussy," I teased him, and finally he did laugh, but weakly, because in a few days I would leave him. I was off to commence the whole life I had before me and move away again, this time to England, which is surrounded by water too, only you can't really surf there like you can in California and Florida, and you'd be surprised at how homesick an unsurfable ocean makes you when you're used to the other kind.

Up until then I had never even owned a coat; all I had was one pair of jeans and twenty pairs of shorts, and I rarely wore shoes. I'd fish for blowfish off the Melbourne Beach pier barefoot. I keep thinking about that these days, about how I hardly ever wore shoes when I lived in Florida even though the concrete they used to lay the pavement was mixed with broken seashells. That pavement reminded me of the Terrazzo floors my mother was so proud of in our home at the time, which, of course, was rented. She always said that when she finally got around to buying her own home, she would have those floors installed. I myself never understood the appeal of Terrazzo floors because to me they looked like they were made from melted bowling balls.

My mother never got around to owning her own home, let alone one with her own Terrazzo floors. She died in a modest cottage surrounded by water right there next to a fishing pier in San Diego. Here she was, a Southern gal who couldn't swim, dying by the ocean after having raised a surfer girl who in turn would give birth to a Southern girl. I'd laugh at the full circle except I don't have a lot of time to reflect these days. And if I did, I wouldn't laugh at that but at how I became a girl who went from never having a home of her own to one who had too many, with none of them near water, yet all of them crying.

The Good Sister

Too Tough To Die

THIS IS MY SECOND TIME TO TOMBSTONE, Arizona, which shouldn't be a surprise, as this is a family trip, and graveyards have always been a big draw for my family. Some of my fondest childhood reflections were of those times when my mother packed us all into the family Fairlane and off we headed to the local cemetery to watch the deer eat flowers off the fresh graves. Good times.

Anyway, Tombstone bills itself as the place "too tough to die," and you gotta admit, for a place hardly bigger than a few city blocks situated smack in the middle of the giant-ass dust basket of the Arizona desert, it's fairly astounding that it's still around. It's the cactus of little towns—not the flower, mind you, because flowers die—but the *cactus*. By all accounts, it should have shriveled up and croaked long ago, but it survived on its own bloody notoriety as a roadside attraction, of sorts, for those traveling between Tucson and Bisbee. FAMOUS GUNFIGHT SITE OF THE O.K. CORRAL! billboards blared. The nearby Boothill Cemetery drew attention, too. Years had to pass for that to happen, though, as the old dead are a lot more acceptable as a tourism curiosity then the fresh dead; For example, you can't really charge money to see the fresh dead, that's something you just have to luck into during your daily activities.

So the road to Tombstone stayed open, and the people here nurtured that tiny tributary with what they had: a gunfight site, a graveyard, a few former brothels turned bar-and-grills, and gift shops that sell re-creations of authentic ad bills, such as the 1881 Boothill Cemetery advertisement that boasts, WHY WALK AROUND HALF DEAD WHEN WE CAN BURY YOU FOR ONLY $22.00? One by one, the people stopped by and a lot of them stayed, many of them exactly the kind of outcast you'd expect to be attracted to a place like this—the handle-bar-mustache, silver-spur-wearing saloon-keeper kind. So Tombstone grew, but not too much, and today it's a lovely little enclave to visit.

I'm here to spend Thanksgiving at the home of my brother, Jim, to whom I've hardly spoken in years. Kim, to whom I talk all the time, insisted I could afford to extract myself from my landlord duties now that I've gotten my rental property to a workable calm. I tried to get out of it, but unsuccessfully. I'm reminded of when we were kids and our parents used to assign a "manners monitor" to the dinner table, someone who would remind us to keep our elbows off the table and not chew like a chimpanzee. Kim made the best manners monitor, so she was assigned the duty a lot. When our father died it happened suddenly, and we were all too young to behave horribly toward each other. Then our mother went and died a slower death just a decade later, just as we were blossoming into maturity but still not mature enough to keep from blaming each other for her sufferings, and that type of pain and blame will last forever if you let it. Believe me, I was the worst offender.

Kim kept communication open between us, intervening every time one of us was in danger of estranging ourselves from the other forever. In short, she is still our manners monitor. She practically had to stick a hook in my tongue and drag me to Nicaragua to see our sister Cheryl, who probably moved there to get away from us. But I've

The Good Sister

been back on my own twice since. It turns out I love that place and I still love my big sister, too.

Jim lives near Tombstone in a town called St. David, Arizona. He moved to the middle of the Arizona desert years ago to be near his wife's parents, who had moved there to retire. I always thought these desert retirement communities were weirdly like those far-off lairs where old elephants go to die, but I might be wrong. Sick old elephants don't play golf all day, for one, and they don't host pool-house mixers every third Thursday, either. So, though I'm not sold on the idea, I'm at least open to the possibility that by the time I'm a hundred years old, the idea of a Tuesday-night doily circle might seem enticing, especially since I hope to spend those years hopped up on morphine.

Anyway, here we all are, together again by Kim's insistence, doing the family thing. I usually act like it's a big bother, but now I realize the bigger bother is keeping up the act. My brother's house is off a dirt road next to a strange oasis of orchard trees owned by his neighbor. Other than that there is nothing around. When he comes out to greet us, from our vantage, with the sun setting on the empty landscape in the distance, we are the only people on earth. Everybody hugs, and Kim can breathe easier. She has done her job, she has kept our connections open, and love can survive like that. It really can. All it needs is just a tiny tributary. Then, as long as you keep the road open, you can nurture it with what you have, no matter how meager that offering may seem. Because love ain't no flower, believe me. It's tougher than that. Love is a *cactus*.

THE CRAZY SISTER

My big sister, Cheryl, has been working since she was fourteen, mostly in service to others, including, but not limited to, various unmotivated live-in boyfriends. Today she owns a bar in Nicaragua, having been afflicted with both our father's wanderlust and our mother's distrust of anything corporate. Cheryl is still making me feel guilty for stealing her bikini two decades ago. But that was small potatoes compared to her nearly stealing Lary, one of the few lunatics—besides Cheryl, of course—who I can't live without.

Heavy Baggage

GRANT AND LARY WEREN'T AT ALL SURPRISED to hear that Cheryl wanted me to haul an actual iron safe to her all the way to Nicaragua. They remember, for example, the last time she came to visit me here in the States. She showed up with no driver's license, no credit card, and no cash—but she had eight heavy hammocks with her, the kind woven with wood frames and bulky macramé.

"Can I borrow some shoes?" she asked as we waited for her hammock-laden luggage, which appeared an hour later in the off-size luggage area, "and, you know, clothes and stuff?"

Thus commenced the visit during which Cheryl moved into my life with all her heavy baggage and, in short, shit on my head for six solid weeks. One of the first things she did was commandeer my eBay account. I still get e-mails from merchants thinking they're contacting her with the latest features of the Waring Pro 1800 Watt Industrial Deep Fryer. It now has a breakaway cord, I'm told, better to keep from killing yourself horribly in a grease fire, and "it's on the heavy side, but shipping to Nicaragua won't be a problem because didn't you say you have a sister who works for an airline? All she has to do is . . ." So a safe is nothing.

Our other sister, Kim, says I just like to complain. Kim arranged our family trip to Nicaragua, and hauled her husband's grown son out here all the way from Geneva, Switzerland, too, because family is important to her. She is always doing that—making sure we all keep in touch and are abreast of each other's lives. If it were not for Kim,

I'd probably be living in some kind of self-inflicted witness-protection program, wary of retrieving my daily paper in case relatives were lurking in the bushes wanting to reattach family ties.

It's a heavy yoke to have inherited. My own mother completely cut herself off from her own six siblings by the time I was five, and any memories I have of them are murky and include aftershave and wingtip shoes. She lived within ten miles of her brother during the last decade of her life, completely unbeknownst to him. I'm not surprised they didn't run into each other, though, seeing as how he was a respectable retired Navy man whose wife hosted poolside appetizer soirees, and my mother was a furloughed weapons specialist whose favorite pastime was stealing patio furniture and digging through dead people's estates. Eventually she became a junk purveyor and went into business with her best friend, Bill, a homeless paranoid conspiracy theorist she met at an auction house as they haggled over a box of broken ceramic beagles and tattered throw pillows. Later Bill used my Social Security number to open a business account at a San Diego bank; then he used the money he earned from that business to move to Central America to open a bar and later a small hotel in Nicaragua, where he promptly had a heart attack.

That is what led my sister Cheryl there, and that is where she remains to this day, happily hosting the other expats at a corner bar called Zoom's. I really thought I'd get away with never having to go there, but she won't move home, so Kim arranged for this here family trip. But before we leave there is the list of provisions we must fill, as to hear Cher say it she lives in a country where supermarkets are stocked like looted convenience stores.

The Crazy Sister

"I have so little problem saying no to the safe," I tell Kim. "I've already got seven pounds worth of chocolate I'm lugging over there; why don't I just put a handle on my house and heave that over while I'm at it?"

Kim herself is a notoriously heavy packer—she has one suitcase that is bigger than my bathroom—but she says she's working on that. When they visited me last New Year's, they were one or two suitcases shy of the usual barge load they bring, and I must say I was proud of her, as my motto regarding packing for a trip is, "Put everything you can't live without in a pile, cut it in half, then pack half of that and you'll still have twice as much as you need."

I hate to check luggage, or luggage in general for that matter, or just hauling heavy crap period. Maybe it has to do with all those years working on the plane, dealing with people's panic as they insisted they saw their bag still on the tarmac as the aircraft backed away from the gate. I swear those attacks were more from the fear of letting go, like they saw some of themselves left behind. Not that they were wrong, but whatter ya gonna do? No matter how heavy your luggage is, what could possibly be in there that can't be replaced?

"Bring the safe," Kim implores me, her love for her sisters heavy in her voice.

"I ain't bringing no safe," I laugh.

The Bitch Who Stole My Bathing Suit

So, no, I did not come bearing a safe. I brought something bigger and heavier. I brought Lary. Cheryl is crazy about Lary, and Lary is just plain crazy, so they were happy to see each other. "I'm not a safe, but I can stand by your stuff with a stick," Lary promised her when they hugged. Whew. She was so glad to see him I was totally off the hook about the safe for the time being.

A few days prior Lary had been thanking God because he hadn't done anything dangerous yet that day, which really surprised me. I would have thought that doing something dangerous was essential for him to start the morning.

"What the hell are you talking about?" I asked. "You love danger."

"I know, but now I like to put it off until later in the afternoon so I have something to look forward to," he says, smiling. And I swear, he was looking more and more like a big blond, blue-eyed piranha fish these days, like his teeth are just gonna take over. He is my best friend, but still, when he smiles at me, it makes me want to look around my seat to see where he placed the poisonous snake.

Five years ago when Cheryl had first ventured down to Nicaragua, Lary was all set to go there with me. Cheryl had called and implored us to meet her there. "C'mon, you fly free, for chrissakes," she prodded. As a matter of fact, I could not, at that time, fly to Nicagoddamn-ragua for free. I could only get as far as Costa Rica for free,

The Crazy Sister

where I'd have to board a dilapidated, rosary-encrusted death bus for a day and a half to get to Nicaragua.

"Sounds fun!" Lary had said. "If anyone kidnaps us, we can escape by weaving ropes from our own hair to pull each other out of our spider holes."

I must admit that it had sounded fun to me, too, so I said okay. Milly was just a baby then and thus motherhood was still too fresh to immediately overshadow my lust for adventure or, for that matter, to immediately resist Cheryl's historic ability to work the guilt angle regarding that time I stole her stupid bikini.

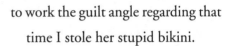

Yes, twenty years ago I stole her stupid bikini and ever since I have been paying for it out my ass. It was the guilt from having thieved her bikini that got me to agree to "ship a few things" for her that she'd left behind in the States after moving to Central America, only to open the storage compartment to discover it was actually a planet-load of crap I was supposed to pack up as well as ship for her. I had to borrow a dented-ass van to haul it all to the airport. In the end it took up an entire cargo compartment and cost me $200—that was with the airline-employee discount.

All because of the bikini. Granted, it was a special bikini that somehow magically made us look like underwear models, but then we were both so young and practically emaciated from our drug-addled pastimes, it was no big feat. Today neither of us could pull that thing past our own toes, but still I'll forever be expected to repay her for that one act of indiscretion. Even Kim, the good sister—as opposed to this crazy one—even *she* occasionally eyes me evenly and says, "Do this for Cher. You did steal her bathing suit, you know." Oh, for chrissakes, she's my sister—if you can't steal from family members, then what good are they?

So, sure, out of force of habit I said okay to Nicaragua at first, but then I immediately backpedaled. By that time Lary had already bought a guidebook, so in the five years since, he's been right up there with the rest of my family, whipping the horses on the bandwagon of guilt to bully me into going down there. "You pussy," he'd bitch. "I bought a guidebook."

So here I am with no excuse anymore, since my airline now flies right into Managua, which is just a whiplash of a taxi ride from Granada, where Cher lives. On top of it Kim corralled family from all over the globe to convene there for a reunion of sorts, and it fell to me to bring the safe. But I brought Lary instead. Lary can build her a safe, for chrissakes.

"All I need is the bottom half of a bus and a fresh pair of pink underpanties," Lary insists as he belts back shots of the local rotgut Cher serves at her bar. Cher knows those are Lary's main ingredients for building anything, so she laughs and throws her arms up to introduce us to the sun-puckered cadre of local expatriates who make up her regular clientele. "Everybody, this is Lary and this," she hollers, hugging me, "*this* is the bitch who stole my bathing suit!"

The Crazy Sister

Lary Land

//

NOW LARY WANTS TO BUY AN ISLAND, as if he doesn't live on one already—just not the kind surrounded by water. It's the kind surrounded by stuff that is not at all like the stuff that makes up his ancient home, which is almost solid concrete, with towering walls made from blocks of the cinder and glass variety, held together by Lary's patented amalgam of, probably, ground-up insects and old cobwebs.

It used to stand by itself on a stretch of highway immediately south of downtown, surrounded by nothing but city views and an old funeral home in the distance, where the smoke from incinerated loved ones belched forth from the chimney. "Ah, home," Lary said to himself each morning as he rolled unconscious crack addicts off his property—"nothing like it."

But in the years since, all the surrounding property has been parceled out and sold to developers. The funeral home was torn down and replaced with a crappy-ass loft complex, and his city view is now dotted with, like, neighbors and stuff, not to mention the houses they live in; brand-new particleboard pieces of crap painted cheery colors like "Sunkissed Peach" and "Mountain Mist." He tried to discourage the yuppies from taking over by wandering his street out front while waving his gun around, but all that did was discourage the real criminals, thus making the neighborhood even more appealing, so he gave up and now there his house sits like a sore, blending in as subtly as a cockroach in a bowl of dinner mints.

So I should have known better than to bring him to Nicaragua. First, Nicaragua is packed with crusty expatriates and other fugitives who do nothing, it seems, but sit in bars ruminating global conspiracy. Second, young Nicaraguan women seem to have no qualms about having regular sex with this gaggle of outcast hermit crabs, and third, you can buy an actual island there for just twenty-five thousand dollars. What was I thinking? This place is Lary Land! The minute we got out of the cab they practically crowned him king.

If there is anyone who can forge a home in a massive lake at the base of volcano in a third-world country, it's Lary. He'd have the whole thing up and running like the Swiss Family Robinson ride at Disney World, only real. He'd figure out how to harness energy from the plumbing system he'll carve from the rocks in tribute to the ancient Roman aqueducts, then fashion automated fishing systems that function in accordance with the lunar cycles; then he'll pirate signals from a satellite when he wants to connect to the rest of the world, and he can do it drunk plus hopped up on whatever discounted local narcotic the populace is derided for exporting to inner-city American drug dealers. Already, while we were at the shantytown of tents that make up the local *mercado*, Lary was demanding I ask the hardware merchant how much it cost for a cluster of rusty elbow valves.

The Crazy Sister

"Stop it! You can get that in the States," I said. "Why aren't you over here looking at this here bloody hog head?" I swear, what was the point of bringing him all that way if he can't inspect a bloody hog head with me? That right there is culture, dammit, and Lary needed to be by my side so we could ridicule it together. "Maybe you can inject it with polypropylene and prop it on a big stick outside your house," I suggested, but even the prospect of a homespun gargoyle didn't drag his attention away from the rusty gadget guy.

"Ask him how much it costs for a concrete block," Lary demanded of me.

"What?" I asked. "How the hell're you gonna drag home a concrete . . ."

Then it hit me. Oh, duh, he's not coming home at all! He wants to stay here for the rest of his life, and who can blame him? Oh, my God, what have I done? I brought my best friend, who happens to be a drunk-ass, drug-grubbing misanthropic old blowfish who likes to build castles out of paper clips and concrete (pretty much), to a far-off land where islands are for the taking, booze is cheap, drugs are plentiful, and sex is noncommittal.

"He says concrete blocks are really expensive," I said desperately. "Really, doncha wanna look at the bloody hog head? You can see his brains through his eye sockets."

That distracted him, but who knows for how long. The next day, back in Granada at my sister's bar, Lary fell into conversation with some of the other societal outcasts, sharing with them his theory that all things are shrinking. "Even measuring tapes, so you can't trust them, either," he insisted, all the while sucking back the locally bot-tled battery acid that is Nicaragua's native rum. Everybody practically patted him on the back, as if to literally take him into their fold. I was watching all this from outside as I caught a cab to the Managua airport. I was leaving to go back to Atlanta, and Lary was not.

"I'm gonna hang here for a few more days," he'd said. "Don't worry, I'll come back soon." Soon, right, I thought as the taxi drove off and I watched Lary's figure diminish in the distance. No one knows how the word *soon* translates in Lary Land.

The Crazy Sister

Lary Is Missing

LORD JESUS GOD, LARY'S MISSING.

Not in the official sense, but in the nobody-knows-where-he-is sense. "Where the hell is Lary?" I screamed at Grant, who inexplicably let me drone on for ten minutes about my cell phone problems before I realized what I was doing. "Why'd you let me go on and on like that?" I cried.

Lary would never let me bloviate for ten minutes about a phone, for chrissake. I couldn't get four sentences into it before he'd start reassembling his rifle. "No, seriously, think about what I'm saying," I remember appealing to him over my Mama Cass theory about how she was no less cool than Jimi Hendrix just because she died choking on a sandwich rather than her own vomit. "We're just talking degrees of digestion here, aren't we?" I whimpered as he ran me out the door waving an exposed electrical wire.

Lary has the sensibilities of a hammerhead shark, which is an essential ingredient to any group of friends; otherwise, it all just goes to hell. Grant loves women too much to threaten me with death if I don't deliver on entertainment, and Daniel just plain loves me too much to shut my ass up when I become boring, but Lary . . . Lary is thoroughly unencumbered by any need to be polite. "Bitch," he'll interrupt, "be interesting or shut up."

But Lary's not around to reboot my brain. Usually I can last pretty long in his absence, but he's been gone for, like, ever. "Where the hell is Lary?" I finally e-mailed my sister, and that is saying something, because Cheryl just got an e-mail address and still treats the computer as though it's a mystical fulcrum possessed by the souls of dead relatives. True to form, though, she was high on drama and sparse on detail. "I think Lary got kicked out of Nicaragua," she said. "I don't know what the big deal was, the other guy didn't even die."

"Where the hell are you!" I e-mailed Lary, and that is saying something, because Lary never bothers with e-mail. He still has an old Mindspring account from way back when the Internet was nothing more than a morass of elbow valves populated by rats with notes tied to their backs. "You fuckup, get the hell home right now. The place is falling apart without you. We don't know who we are. Grant and I have no criteria against which to compare ourselves. Without you here to pollinate the air with your insanity molecules, we're just bumping into each other like farty fools. Come home. Now."

Notice how I dragged Grant into this, because if it were just me in crisis, Lary would take his sweet time responding. In reality, Grant is about as shook up over Lary's absence as a brick of petrified poo. But me, I'm in serious danger. The last time Lary disappeared, it was when he went to Germany to manage a rock band for half a year. When he came back, I was married to a geologist and living on a cul-de-sac in Roswell.

"Christ," I exclaimed when he finally called, "see what happens when you leave me alone?"

He almost had to employ his experimental dead-body-mulching breakthrough to get me out of that one. But thankfully no corpses were in need of disposal that time, as my hapless new husband was as

The Crazy Sister

happy to see me go as I was to touch turf on the concrete floor of the dilapidated warehouse Lary calls home.

Amazingly Lary e-mailed me back yesterday. It turns out he's now living on a ship somewhere off the coast of Nicaragua, which is owned by his friend's ex-girlfriend's sister's husband and must be equipped with some form of spacecraft satellite receptors, as now Lary keeps sending me pictures of his finger pointing out coordinates on a map. "This is where I am," his e-mail says, "no cars, no motorcycles, no bicycles, just a small private island with a big crescent beach. My ass is staying put, so don't bother looking for me. As for criteria against which to compare yourselves, check out some of the early Japanese sci-fi radioactive mutants."

Oh, gawd, it's happening, it's starting. Lary has sailed off into the damn sunset and now he's gonna be one of those human barnacles you see on islands in the Caribbean living under lean-tos made out of bent beer cans and old umbrella handles. I knew it. We all wondered what the hell he was doing here, anyway, in the city, when he has that head full of wild blond straw for hair and skin as brown as a suitcase abandoned at a bus stop.

"Get your ass back here!" I hollered at him as loud as you can holler over e-mail.

But the answer that came was forebodingly guileless for Lary. "I will come home," he said, "when I have a good reason."

Pathetic Howling

MY CAT JETHRO IS MISSING AGAIN, and this time Lary cannot have taken him because Lary is still missing, too. But that doesn't keep me from accusing Lary of kidnapping my cat. He loves Jethro, and the last time he threatened to kidnap him was just a few months before he disappeared. "You think your door can keep me out?" he laughed. "I'd have that thing unlocked before I put my car in park."

So I spent the first day Jethro was missing assuming it was all a bad joke. "Gimme back my cat, you polluted raccoon! You're playing with my feelings here," I cried into Lary's e-mail. Usually such flirting merits a return response within the hour, but Lary took his time because he was at that moment soaking in a Jacuzzi of high-grade tequila on a tiny island off the coast of Central America.

"I don't have your cat," he e-mailed me the next day. "But you better find him because I love that cat."

Nobody argues that Jethro is a magical cat, and the fact that Lary agrees is testimony because Lary warms to animals like a blowtorch to a toilet brush. His last cat, Cocksucker, who was foisted on him by a sympathetic friend who felt Lary could use a bit of warm-bloodedness in his life, didn't even qualify for the occasional head pat. No wonder the poor thing died mysteriously one morning after eating his fourth can of Fancy Feast. Of course I blamed Lary.

"Listen," Lary insisted, "Cocksucker died because he was a cocksucker. He probably keeled over because his crustiness finally froze up his heart."

The Crazy Sister

Not that Lary isn't fully capable of slaughtering the innocent, but in the case of Cocksucker, Lary might have a point. I could see how that cat could have died out of sheer orneriness. Cocksucker really was evil, for one, and older than magma, and Lord that cat was ugly, too. He had eyes the color of frozen gunmetal, tobacco-colored teeth, and a hide so wiry you could use him to wash your pots. His sole activity seemed to be to sit by his bowl glaring and growling, and not the normal injured-moose kind of growl you'd expect from a feline but the kind of growl that grizzly bears make. You really started to wonder, after a while, if he wasn't a cat at all but one of Attila's more bloodthirsty Huns living out an eternal curse of some kind. In all, the cat was about as approachable as a coiled cobra and it's a wonder he lasted as long as he did.

Now that Cocksucker's gone, though, Lary keeps bugging me to give him Jethro, my magical big, fat yellow cat, my big ball of love, my king-size pillow covered in soft fur the color of sunlight. When I hug him, he purrs in my ear and I'd never let him go if I could help it. Maybe it's his gentle nature or lumbering physique or serene green eyes, but there is something about Jethro that is incandescently loveable. I adopted him after one glimpse at a cell phone photo, and he was barely through my door before Keiger, who is normally as demonstrative as a redwood, exclaimed, "Now that's a good cat." Even Lary—Lary, who is about as loveable as a sewer rat—loves him. So when I came home to find Jethro disappeared, I of course thought Lary took him. But even I had to conclude after a while that it would be pretty impossible for Lary to kidnap my cat from a sailboat off the coast of Central America.

So once that finally sank in, I flew outside and began knocking on doors. The entire time I've lived here I've only met my neighbors on either side, but it turns out that Jethro has been busier than me and had spent a lot of time canvassing the neighborhood acting as ambassador on my behalf. "That's your cat? I love that cat. He was just here," was the popular response from neighbors who'd called after reading my flyer. Jethro was not an indoor cat, which is one of the reasons I moved into the tiny house with the big backyard.

The house is blue with aluminum awnings, and so small it reminded me of the trailers my dad used to sell, or *try* to sell. If my dad had been as good at selling trailers as he was at *talking* about selling trailers with his buddies at the bar, we might never have had Missy, the closest thing I'd ever had to my own pet cat as a kid. My dad found the calico howling pathetically behind the Dumpster one night as he made his way back to the car after the bar closed. Missy spawned a half dozen kittens about five days later, and a month or two after that my mother took off work to bring them to my first-grade class in a cardboard box for show-and-tell. "They're ready for adoption," she chirped. That's how I learned the definition

The Crazy Sister

of "adoption," which directly translated into the ripping of six little furry hearts from my six-year-old chest.

I howled every time I came home to discover another kitten vanished. I rolled around on the floor at my mother's feet, wailing, begging her to tell me where they'd gone so I could get them back. She simply lit another Salem menthol, turned on the television, and tried to ignore me. I could see her cigarette shake, though, as she brought it to her lips.

"Where the hell is my cat?" I kept hollering into Lary's voicemail. But the exclamation had become more of a pathetic howl than a question. But sometimes howling can twang the most unexpected heart chords.

Who knows, maybe Lary was sick of sitting around in paradise surrounded by beauty when there was a world of ugliness waiting for him back here in Atlanta. Maybe he'd humped one too many local damsels and finally infuriated the machismo populace. Maybe he'd finally formed that revolutionary army to overtake the government and felt his duty was done—whatever it was, all I know is that after hearing my wretched noise one too many times, Lary flew home to launch his own determined search for Jethro.

I didn't even know Lary was back until he called me and I cried, "Where's my cat?" and he answered, "I have him right here." He had found Jethro down the street in a vacant lot under a bush, barely breathing, sick from renal failure. He must have been hidden there for days. When Lary gathered him up and brought him back to me, the most I could hope for was a goodbye before Jethro's sweet heart stopped beating.

Lord Jesus God, I wish Jethro had it in him to howl like I do, but instead he tried to die without saying goodbye or being a bother at all. Still sometimes I wake up thinking I remember I did hear howling. I wake up and I think, *Was that Jethro?* Sometimes I'll call Lary. "It wasn't Jethro," he'll say, "it was just you again."

The Crazy Sister

Tequila Lary

Now that Lary is finally home from Nicaragua, he keeps saying the strangest things, such as, "It feels good to be human again," as though that's what he was *before* he went to Nicaragua. Though, oddly, Cheryl says he acted human the whole time.

"I swear," she said. "He sat at the same table with my family and didn't break a chair over anyone's head or anything."

That's pretty astounding, and the only explanation I can think of is it sounds like Tequila Lary struck again. Tequila, after all, is the most notorious of all behavior-altering alcohols. I consider myself an expert on this subject, seeing as how I used to live in a trailer park two miles north of the Tijuana border. It's noted, fairly, that in the past I've proclaimed myself an expert on a lot of things for this same reason, but I'm serious this time. It's the tequila, I'm telling you, and the fact that I lived in such close proximity of the country where it's made, that burdens me with this knowledge.

First, it was literally cheaper than water to buy your tequila supply in Mexico rather than to brave your fake ID at an American liquor store in my neighborhood. So mix that with some audacious kids in a Baja bug, and that right there is nothing but a big recipe for prom vomit. I remember one football game my freshman year when I got so drunk I had to leave the bleachers fifty times to stand in line at the toilet. The next morning I woke up with a bunch of strange hair caught in my watchband. Soon my roommates recounted, to my horror, how I'd steadied my progression through the bleachers by grabbing the tops of the heads of the other spectators on either side, as if they were all just human knobs on a big balustrade.

Regardless, I made a ton of friends that night, because tequila altered my behavior to the point where I was evidently a lot of fun to be around. I remember thinking I better stay away from that stuff, because I didn't want to give people the impression that's what I was really like. To be constantly like that—all outgoing and able to charm people out of being pissed at me for pulling out their hair with my watchband—would be an effort beyond my ability to fathom.

When Cheryl drinks tequila, she practically shoots acid out her eye sockets. Seriously, you do not want to be within swinging distance of that girl after one too many shots. One night in college, after a pitcher of margaritas, she hit me over the head with a potted palm tree. "Did I do that to you?" she whimpered as she held my hand while the doctor bandaged my head the next day.

"Hell yes, bitch! Lay off the tequila," I hollered. But no one could convince her to quit until she bought her own bar and simply tired of the stuff after watching her patrons transform into drunk, ass-itching spider monkeys night after night. When Lary was there, amazingly, he hardly tore the place apart at all. He simply sat on the end stool and quietly played buffer to all the other crazies in the place. My sister, who has known Lary for more than a decade, couldn't believe it. "Is he all right?" she asked me.

"Are you feeding him tequila?" I asked. "Because you gotta stop doing that. Tequila Lary creeps us out. He's all polite and asks how you are and acts interested in the answer."

The Crazy Sister

But she *didn't* stop. She kept him plied and then got him to help her cocktail waitresses move her furniture and fix the saloon doors that lead to the leaky toilet. "I love Tequila Lary," she proclaimed.

"No, what you want is *Jäger* Lary," I insisted. "Jäger Lary would have stolen you some new furniture, impregnated your waitresses, and installed a camera in your toilet. That's the Lary I know and love," I said. But she was too busy admiring his work to fear the complete breakdown in civil order that I predicted would occur if Lary continued to be polite and considerate.

Which he will do—because he brought boxes of tequila back fresh from the duty-free counter at the airport. "Did you know they make a tequila liqueur now? [sip, sip] It's my new medicine. [sip, sip] I missed you, by the way. How was your holiday?" he asked. The scary part is that he actually sounded interested.

Dead Hooker

I'VE BEEN WEIGHING THE COST OF HOMICIDE lately, wondering if it might be worth it in the long run. Of course I dream all the time about killing my overexcited sister Cheryl—who has appeared from Nicaragua to squat in my life again. But the dreams aren't that satisfying. For one, there's all that remorse. "Dang, why did I do that?" I remember thinking in my dream, my dead sister at my feet. "I stained my favorite shirt, and now I have to dispose of the body."

Lary has often offered me his cleanup services in this regard. After a lifetime of pensive research, foolproof body disposal is supposedly something he's finally figured out, and he's eager to put his theory to work. For example, he likes to remind me that he's the one to call if I ever wake up with a dead hooker in my hotel room.

"Why the hell would there be a dead hooker in my hotel room?" I ask.

"You never know," he says, his teeth gleaming.

At first I thought the probability was pretty slim, but then I realized you don't have to actually *hire* a hooker to have her end up dead in your hotel room. Who knows, she could have knocked on your door after huffing too much glue and died right there by the luggage stand

The Crazy Sister

with you as the hapless bystander. It's possible. I've known plenty of hookers in my day, and not all of them limited to the crack whores who used to populate my neighborhood. Some of them worked at the same steakhouse with my sister back in San Diego, and that restaurant was located in the lobby of an actual hotel, which made it pretty convenient. None of them ended up dead, though, that I know of.

I worked there myself one summer. Cheryl and I said we were twenty and twenty-two, respectively, when really I was seventeen and she was nineteen. Until then I'd made money sewing the uniforms for the girls, which was a cake job if there ever was one, because the skirt portion took so little material I could make them out of cut-up pillowcases if I wanted. It was the aprons that were difficult. They had to be exactly ten inches in length with a dozen pockets and a Velcro waistband, all tailored with pleats, yet lie flat enough so as not to tilt them as they teetered on their come-fuck-me pumps and wagged their asses in the faces of the patronage, 90 percent of which were airline pilots and rich criminals.

It was the dinner shift that was notorious for its line of call girls working the tables, so it's not surprising that many of the dinner girls got caught "working the box," as Cheryl put it. There'd been an actual raid a few years prior, and many were prosecuted to little avail, so by the time I'd started there the girls had figured out how to get creative with their payment demands. One waitress worked the box for rent checks and others for car payments, and all of them had eyes as dead as nail heads.

My sister worked the lunch shift rather than the box, but she still made so much money it should have been outlawed for a girl her age, what with her penchant for unemployed boyfriends, to have so much cash on hand. I worked the breakfast shift, a time of day usually shunned by the playboys known to frequent the place, so most of my customers were clueless hotel guests who'd wandered in expecting regular coffee-shop fare. The restaurant was void of even a single ray of natural light, so I spent most of my shifts trying to read the newspaper with the pin lamp the bartender kept by the cash register.

The place had gold-and-red brocade wallpaper, booths upholstered in red vinyl, and menus that were made—I swear this is true—of actual red meat. Every morning the cook covered serving platters with decorative lettuce and laid slabs of raw steak on top, and it was our job to carry these to the tables and point to each piece like a prize on a game show. "And here you have your aged, Angus-farmed filet mignon . . ." When I left at noon, blinded by sunlight but relieved to be free, I'd run to my car with my arms outstretched. After a few months I tried to get fired by revealing my real age to the owner, a Sasquatch of a man in a red satin shirt unbuttoned to his nipples. I thought for sure he'd fire me, as I was too young to serve alcohol, and even in the morning there were a lot of boozers in there. But he just shrugged and told me to be sure to pick out all the red cabbage from his salad before serving it to him.

So before long I started picking up a lunch shift here and there, started making real money, started getting used to it, started thinking maybe I didn't need to go to college after all. Then one day a customer asked me if I wanted my rent paid, and my sister intervened. "Watch it, that's my little sister," she told the guy. After that she implored me

The Crazy Sister

to leave the job and never come back. She must have known that if I kept this up, I'd be in trouble. If I kept this up—with the darkness, smoke, and gold brocade—in no time at all I'd have eyes as dead as nail heads.

A Heavy Head

CHERYL FLEW HOME TO VISIT KIM, even though she doesn't consider anywhere in America home anymore. And from there she called me, of course, when she needed help shipping her new moose head back to Central America. "I tell you, in the long run it's cheaper to just pay the imported prices and just buy the stuff down there," I told her, "because no matter how cheap it is here, the shipping costs are going to kill you."

"But they don't have moose in Nicaragua," Cheryl whined.

"They don't have moose in Dayton goddamn Ohio, either," I reminded her, as Dayton is where Kim lives and where Cheryl is staying. "Why the hell do you want a moose head?"

"Because it's a mechanical talking moose head," she hollered. "It'll be great! C'mon, Hollis. It only weighs sixty pounds."

"Jesus, Cher, just move home, for God's sake," I said. "It costs a hell of a lot less to ship moose heads domestically."

"I told you they don't have moose heads in Nicaragua," she said. And it took me a second before I realized that, by hearing me tell her to move home, Cher thought I'd told her to return to Granada, as that's where she now considered *home*. I was stunned.

"I mean *here* home," I said.

The United States was her home—wasn't it? Cheryl didn't seem concerned about that; she was instead describing the many attributes of a robot moose head and how it would increase the patronage at her bar.

The Crazy Sister

It has been five years since Cheryl moved to Nicaragua, where she lives with her new husband, Wayne. They met in a bar in Las Vegas, where she worked as a casino cocktail waitress and he worked "in distribution," whatever that means. When Cheryl first introduced me to Wayne, he had a hairdo that was popular among many second-rate stage magicians at the time—a blond mullet that cascaded down his back and could touch the belt looped through the waist of his acid-washed denim parachute pants. By the time they married, the mullet was gone, thankfully.

"A moose head can't be that hard to ship to Nicaragua," Cheryl insisted, and I realized she has a history of insisting things are easy when they're not. She drove her truck to Nicaragua, for example. Just pointed it south and hit the gas until she arrived. It was easy, she insists, though I know it couldn't have been.

"C'mon," she continued, "sixty pounds can't be that heavy."

"Believe me," I said, "that head is heavier than you think it is."

Even *squirrel* heads are heavier than you think they are. I know this because just yesterday I stepped on a squirrel brain that my new cat, Petal, left for me on my bedroom rug. I would have been disgusted, but my disgust was outweighed by admiration for Petal, who had somehow extracted the brain completely intact from the squirrel's

head, which itself I'd found a few days prior, also neatly sitting on the '70s-era rug I keep at the base of my bed. I love this rug. I've sold things on eBay before, things that were featured in photographs near this rug, only to be inundated with requests to buy the rug and not the item. Petal, a feline Hannibal Lector we acquired to replace the gentle Jethro, must know this is my favorite, as she constantly leaves me these little presents—a squirrel head here, a dead bird there, a lizard torso—right where she knows I'll find them. I can't freak out or anything, as I know they're left with love; to a cat a squirrel brain is a delicacy.

My sister feels the same way about fish cheeks. I discovered this one night in Nicaragua, when she made me order the local seafood. "Eat the cheeks! Eat the cheeks!" she adamantly insisted.

"Are you talking about the gills?" I asked, because who would eat fish gills? That's like eating nostrils. The fish came fried and sitting upright on a colorful ceramic plate, and it was the ugliest fish I had ever seen. I think it even had teeth and hair.

"Taste it," Cher growled when she saw me hesitate. She was almost using her scary voice. So I poked at the fish and took a tiny taste. After all, I guess I owed her one.

Years earlier while I was living with our mother in Switzerland, Cheryl was shacking up with her third progressively worse boyfriend (as far as our mother was concerned). Our mother refused to support Cheryl financially if Cheryl was supporting someone else financially, and Cheryl always seemed to be supporting someone else financially. She was, after all, my mother's daughter.

So when our mother had gotten the job in Switzerland, she chose *me* to take with her. I was working as a part-time receptionist at a real-estate brokerage and had set a pattern of forsaking personal

The Crazy Sister

relationships in favor of adventure and other pursuits, like college. In fact, I'd just gotten my degree in writing from an expensive private university. ("This will come in handy when you get that job selling Xerox copiers," the professor had told me as he handed me my diploma.) And my mother wanted to make sure I didn't shit it away. "Live with me for a year and you can write articles and get published in magazines," she implored, so I did and I did. Today I am able to cobble together a burgeoning career as a writer while my airline is going bankrupt, and Cheryl is the dubiously thrilled proprietor of a Central American bar she runs with Wayne, who I have not seen sober since they moved there almost five years ago.

The fish, by the way, was the best thing I ever tasted.

"I knew it," Cheryl said, her voice taking a softer tone.

Sometimes I wonder how it would have turned out if Cheryl had gone to Switzerland instead of me, how she might have fared if she'd been able to utilize that gift I'd been bestowed during that time. Often I long to talk to her about this, but I never do. Instead, with heavy head, I turn away and remain silent.

She Knows

SOMETIMES I FEEL BAD ABOUT ABANDONING Cheryl at the Vancouver airport, but mostly I just think Vancouver is a hell of a great place to be abandoned in and she can damn well deal with it. I'd even warned her. "If there's a single seat on that plane home and it's a choice between you and me, I am grabbing it. I'll be waving to you from the window as we take off, I swear I will."

I didn't have time to dick around on the way home like I did on the way there, a journey that took us three days, two hotel rooms, and a rental car. I hadn't meant to come to Vancouver, but I promised my brother-in-law Eddie that for his birthday I'd take Cheryl far away. I heard they have moose in Canada, and I thought it would be fun for us to see a real one for the first time, as opposed to the fake one she shipped air freight at a cost equivalent to the purchase of a whole herd. Her visit with Eddie and Kim had been going on for four months, which made me marvel at their patience. Cheryl hardly drinks at all anymore, so at least there's that huge improvement, but still there's the other things, the little things, the collection of idiosyncrasies our sister possesses that makes hosting her over a long period of time fairly maddening.

For one, she doesn't seem capable of speaking in normal tones, only in excitable bursts, and after a while it gets a little exhausting to be in the presence of a person whose excitement level constantly has the intensity of a crowd of people miraculously healed at a religious revival.

Then there is the fact that, since she moved to a third-world country just five years ago, her brain seems to have been sucked clean of

The Crazy Sister

any memory of modern convenience. For example, I know she knew there was such a thing as computers before she left to live in Central America, and I even know there are lots and lots of computers actually existing in Granada as we speak, as I've been there and seen them—there's an Internet cafe across the street from the tavern she owns, for chrissakes—but still Cheryl looks at my laptop like it's a shiny object she wants to break open against a rock to see what's inside.

And how do you live on Planet Earth and not know how to use an ATM? Cheryl has had a bank account since she was fourteen; I've seen her use an ATM many times. But now she'll approach one and say, with panic rising in her voice, "It says 'enter your PIN number.' What's a PIN number? What does it mean, *enter?* Is there an opening where you put it?"

It's the little things like this that send me over the edge. Sometimes I wonder if she knows.

On the way to Canada, it was supposed to have been one simple five-hour flight, but we were flying standby on my friend's airline-employee buddy passes, which is a surefire way to fuck up your plans if you're fool enough to make any. If you've ever flown on a buddy pass, then I don't have to tell you your best bet is to simply appear at the airport with a bull's-eye painted on the back of your pants and tell the ticket agent to direct you to the tarmac where, if you're extremely lucky, you might get a few planes to ass-ram you within a day's driving distance of your destination. I had warned Cheryl about this, but she was undeterred.

"I've got time," she said wistfully. She was always being wistful about things I felt were fairly serious, like how she'd up and moved to Central

America one day. But as long as she'd been warned that she could get stuck in any number of cities from here to the Pacific, I felt I'd done my job as the fun-sucking sister, and we could commence our meandering adventure. No need to fret over Cheryl, I thought. She knows.

But when it came time to fly home, I was under pressure to get back because I am an actual mother, and my girl was returning from vacation with the big Italian part of her family in New Jersey. Sometimes I'm self-conscious about the fact that most of my own extended family is either dead or doesn't know I exist, which I guess is how my mother wanted it when she decided to cut off communication with them when I was little. Sometimes I wish I had uncles and stuff, but those moments are pretty fleeting and almost entirely isolated to when my daughter returns from vacation in New Jersey spouting stuff like, "My whole family is Italian!" And I have to remind her that I am her mother, which makes me part of her family, and I am not Italian.

But admittedly, when you look at Milly—with her caramel skin and hair and huge brown eyes—you would never know her whole family is not Italian. In contrast, my own eyes are green and I've been saturating my hair with bleach since I was nineteen, when the blond I was born with began to darken. When Milly and I are together, no one ever remarks at our resemblance, which makes me worry sometimes that after these trips away I'll have to remind Milly I'm her mother when we're together again. But that thought dissolves the instant she runs into my arms. She knows.

Cheryl's own looks favor our father. She has his dimples and mischievous eyes, back before his became rheumy with booze and then

The Crazy Sister

dulled with heart disease. I patted her on the shoulder before abandoning her in Vancouver to get back to my girl. As I predicted, the plane had exactly one open seat on it, and true to my word, I grabbed it. It was the very last seat in the cabin, which meant I'd have to spend the flight averting my gaze from all the eye-level crotches standing in line for the lavatory, but I was happy to be aboard.

Once I got situated, I looked up to see that the gate agent had let my sister on board as well, and I got elated there for a while, until I realized she'd talked them into doing a walk-through in case they'd overlooked an empty spot. When they realized they hadn't, they turned her around and escorted her off the plane. As I saw my sister go, in her stained raincoat and hapless rucksack, I suddenly got all overcome. "Christ, am I crying?" I thought. "I can't believe this." Lord Jesus God, I realized, I damn-ass better see Cheryl again, because if the last sight I ever have of my sister is of her being left behind, I seriously don't think I could bear it.

After the plane took off, the flight attendant came back to laugh at Cheryl's antics on the Jetway before they closed the door, which didn't surprise me. Cheryl is one of those super maniacally contagiously smiley kinda people, and there were probably a hundred passengers on that plane at that moment that this flight attendant would have happily left on the Jetway instead. The flight attendant recounted how she extended her sincere regrets to my sister as we were leaving, and offered to deliver me a message if she wanted. At that, the flight attendant told me, Cheryl just grinned as the door was closing and said, "She knows."

My Missing Sister

RUMOR HAS IT THAT CHERYL MADE IT BACK to Nicaragua. We don't know for absolute certain, but Kim reports that Cheryl's bank account shows there was a withdrawal last week from an ATM machine (ha! I knew she knew how to use one!) in Granada, and we figure it must have been made by our sister, since she is the only other person who knows the password, and she wouldn't give it out even if someone threatened to chop off her arms. We know this because that exact threat was made by the last person who tried to rob Cheryl. It was eighteen years ago, and that man is still icing down his balls to this day, probably.

"Cher first paid a two-dollar fee to inquire about her balance," Kim observed, "then she spent another two dollars to make the withdrawal." We found that funny because it was so in keeping with the fact that, no matter what her efforts are to keep from wasting money, Cheryl never fails to waste money. Take last month. It would have cost her $895 for a full-fare ticket to Vancouver, but instead she paid $250 to fly standby. In the end, after reroute fees, hotel rooms for those nights stranded in strange cities on the way to her destination, two rental cars, and one train ticket, she ended up spending close to $1,200 to get there and back. But on that last leg of her trip, when she had to rent a car to get from Cincinnati to her final destination of Kim's house in Dayton, the rental-car clerk, out of the goodness of his heart, upgraded Cheryl to a convertible Mustang at the last minute for no additional fee.

The Crazy Sister

"Yeeeeehaaaawww!" Cheryl hooted into her cell phone as she hurled down the freeway with the wind tossing her hot-pink streaked hair into a tiny tornado above her head. "This car normally cost $150 a day! This makes it all worth it."

"You're missing it," Kim said, and tried to explain further about how it would have been cheaper if Cheryl had just paid the full ticket price. But by then Cheryl had accidentally tossed her cell phone onto the back floorboard while waving to a trucker. She arrived in Dayton an hour later, ready to roost herself in Kim's life for a few more weeks before attempting to travel back to Central America, where we think she made it, based on her bank receipts.

"I missed my flight and I'm stuck in Miami," her last phone message said. "I might make it out tomorrow."

I suppose if anything serious is amiss, we'll hear about it, like if Cheryl really is missing or if she finally killed her husband like she should; and most likely we'll hear about it from Cheryl herself afterward, though Kim always complains that Cheryl never offers any details in her e-mail updates ("I'm leaving Wayne, see you Wednesday!"). But I consider these detail-free missives a definite plus. We don't need to know why Cheryl left her husband, just that it was high time she did. Same for when she went back to him six months later.

Kim, though, needs more details. She has always been that way . . . wanting to know what was on the menu before we decided on a restaurant, what the terms were on the lease before we signed the rental agreement, what was in the syringe before the Guatemalan doctor injected us with it. She is so damn picky. I remember when we took our last family trip to Vegas that my mother had finagled through some time-share Ponzi schemers or something. All we kids had to do to qualify for free hotel rooms—not to mention cocktails—was sit through a three-hour sales presentation in a convention room next to the lobby. Kim was only fifteen, but still she questioned the equity of trading three hours of our time being assaulted by high-pressure salesmen in exchange for a free hotel room when hotel rooms were going for just $25 that weekend anyway. "Not to mention that cocktails in Vegas are already free," she pointed out.

But Cheryl and I were too busy trying to suck down as many tequila sunrises as we could before we had to admit we were underage and not legally liable for anything we signed, at which point my brother became the main morsel of rotting meat for the vultures to peck. To this day he complains that that free hotel room cost him thousands of dollars in useless dues until the time-share profiteering company finally collapsed and couldn't afford to pay their attorneys to extort money from their members anymore.

But at least that tale lives on as part of our family history. My brother just retold it this past Thanksgiving, and we all laughed so hard I thought I was going to cough up all the crayons I ate in kindergarten. "It's worth it just to have the memory," he said.

"No, you're missing it," Kim insisted. "It's cheaper to just pay." And she's right. Once you factor in the time it takes to finagle, the stress of worrying it won't work out, and the credit card charges you rack up once it inevitably doesn't, it's probably always cheaper to just pay. Cheryl, for one, is forever missing that part. She would likely be

The Crazy Sister

more mindful of missing it, I think, if she weren't so busy hopping the globe with the wind whipping through her hair as she cruises down the highway in a surprise convertible Mustang.

Friends & Lovers

I sometimes wonder if we—Daniel, Grant, Lary, Keiger, and me—came together simply because we found each other after we'd been excluded by everyone else. Whatever the case, I bonded to each of them like welded metal. These stories exemplify this bond, even when it looks more like complete exasperation than love. Whatever it may be, we made it our mission to rescue each other, even if, as was often the case, rescue was the last thing we thought we needed.

Begging from the Other Side

I WAS DEFINITELY WEARING THE WRONG CLOTHES for a kidnapping, which is funny, because as a matter of course I'm usually outfitted pretty well for felonious behavior. In middle school, when I broke into ninth-grade heartthrob Tyler Freelander's house, I did not even need to go home to get my gardening gloves. I already had them hanging out of my back pocket when my sister suggested the idea, and off we went. Had the police dusted the place afterward, they'd have found my sister's prints peppered all over the place, while mine would have been nowhere to be found. In the end, the Freelanders never even knew we burgled their home, as our booty consisted solely of one belt buckle and one deck of pornographic playing cards. Had we done it because of greed, we'd have amassed a much bigger haul, I'm sure, but we didn't do it because of that. We did it because of love.

And it was because of love that Grant, Daniel, and I were at Thumbs Up planning a kidnapping. Lary should have been there, definitely, because out of the four of us, he is the only one with actual experience. "Get yer ass over here," Grant bellowed into Lary's voicemail. "You rig shit for a living, we need something rigged. A person. And she probably won't like it. In fact, it'll probably be against her will." Lary must have been indisposed, because he couldn't have resisted otherwise.

"If I'm going to kidnap someone, I'm going to need to change my clothes," I insisted. I was wearing one of my better thrift-store dresses, a satin shift actually, and satin is pretty slippery. It would have been perfect to wear if I were the one getting gripped, but not if I was the one expected to do the gripping. So it was agreed we'd all go home to change before we pounced, and then we'd stop at the hardware store and buy a bunch of plastic tie-downs (which I know make great makeshift handcuffs because that's what we flight attendants once used on the plane to restrain a female passenger who took off all her clothes and wouldn't stop masturbating right in front of the movie screen). But before the three of us could go further we surmised we had to go and get our other friend, Boots. We definitely needed a fourth person, one for each flailing limb, we figured, and Grant had a big quilt he wanted to go home and get in order to use, too, though I still don't know why. He kept talking about a "technique."

"We each hold a corner and kind of come at her," he was explaining, though it still seemed confusing. "Seriously," he continued, insisting that this quilt factored into an official restraint process he'd learned back when he worked at a mental institution for emotionally damaged children. I pointed out that our friend, the one we were kidnapping, the one we love, had also worked at that institution for sixteen years, so she was doubtlessly familiar with the technique and could probably thwart it. He was about to argue with me when he slammed on the brakes instead.

"That's her car!" he shrieked. "There she is!"

I had not seen her in a year. Hardly any of her old friends had. Daniel thought he'd said something to drive her away. Boots kept waiting for her to return her calls. Grant had heard rumors; we all did, snippets here and there. But we were busy balancing the big wads

Friends & Lovers

of petty crap that comprised our own lives to do anything about it. Besides, you don't want to impose, right? And surely she knew she is loved, right? Surely she knew all she had to do is call, or cry, or just show up, knock on the door, come in and collapse in our arms. Surely she knew that.

I'd heard there'd been an arrest, but amazingly I didn't chalk it up to a bad sign, just bad fortune. I'm exasperatingly nonjudgmental that way. *Whoa, what crappy luck,* I remember thinking, *to happen to be at your friend's place, who happens to be a meth dealer, right when the police happen to stage a raid.* Then I heard she was doing the drug, too. Dabbling, I figured. She'll snap out of it. Right.

You have to understand, we are not talking about a typical addict. (Are we?) She was a good mother, with a good job and a lovely home, and a husband who was her college sweetheart, and a daughter—oh my God, a beautiful daughter, a lovely, honey-haired little daughter she rocked in her arms when she was a baby, who lay breathing on her breast like a bundle of warm dough, whose closed lids she kissed with the pure and powerful love of a new mother.

Then a year goes by.

A typical year is nothing, if you think about it, an eye blink in the normal course of events. But crystal meth will take a typical year and put a rocket on it, leaving your life charred and destroyed in its wake. Everything you love, everything you cherish, depleted. Fuel for the rocket. In one year this friend lost her job, husband, house, and daughter. She was spending her nights digging through Dumpsters. When Daniel heard it, he cried like a child, and then galvanized us into some kind of action. We did not have a plan, except that we planned to make a time to meet to make a plan. Then we happened upon her. Just like that. And all of us wearing the wrong clothes for a kidnapping.

"There she is!" Grant shrieked again. "What should we do?"

I swear, when it comes to kidnapping people, Grant cannot possibly be a bigger pussy. I even found myself wishing Lary were there, and I thought my days of longing for Lary's company were behind me, believe me. But Lary was not there, and we could not even reach him by cell phone for more advice. It was just me and Grant and Daniel. We were quite unprepared, really, to come upon our subject so suddenly. There she was, not seeing or expecting us, outside and everything, a perfect opportunity, and all Grant could do is shout, "What should we do? What should we do?" He even passed her by.

"Turn the fuck around!" I hollered. Amazingly, Grant did as I said and turned around, but as we approached her, he still kept shrieking, "What should we do?"

"We're gonna go get her, goddammit," I said with pure conviction. I rarely have pure conviction. Offhand, I'd say the last time I had it was when I snuck into a sold-out Tina Turner concert after my friends kept saying, "You're never gonna get in," and I simply said, "Like hell I'm not." And I crawled over Dumpsters stuffed with trash, and not just any trash, but bad, grubby, disgusting trash full of fish bones and rancid meat and rotting kitten carcasses and stuff like that. But I didn't care because I saw that light, see? I just knew it led where I wanted to go. I had pure conviction.

Friends & Lovers

The window led to the men's toilet backstage, and I hollered to my friends that the coast was clear, begging them from the other side to follow me, but they wouldn't. So I went on alone and ended up in the front row.

"What should we do?" Grant was saying as we watched our friend all out in the open, practically begging to be abducted. "We're not ready." He was right; we weren't ready. But when are you ever ready for this? We weren't exactly ready for the news that our friend had become a meth addict and lost everything dear to her, either. She lost everything, but if you saw her on the street, she'd smile sweetly like she always used to and tell you everything was fine . . . a little fucked up but otherwise fine. And you'd walk away wanting to believe her. I tell you, though, if there is ever one truth to be taken from any of this, it's that addicts lie.

This time we weren't walking away. She was outside the house that is no longer her house, taking furniture from it that might or might not be hers. We don't know. We were told not to believe a word she says. "It's not her talking," we were informed. But it sure was good to hear her voice even if it wasn't her talking. "Everything's fine," she kept saying. She had a drug buddy waiting for her in a car with the engine running, but Grant had (very reluctantly) blocked their exit with his brand-new Honda Element. ("What if my car gets rammed?" he bitched. "Even better," I bitched back.)

The three of us got out and circled around her like a small herd of protective ponies, insisting she come with us. And this is where I'm glad Grant was there and not Lary, as Lary would have simply clouted her over the head with a socket wrench and thrown her in the backseat like a sack of sand. Instead Grant took her by the hand and simply implored her to follow us. "We love you," he kept repeating gently. "Come with us, right now." He spoke with pure conviction, so she got in our car willingly, smiling gamely like a mom being led to a breakfast made by her kids.

When she realized where we were taking her, she dropped the act, though, or perhaps she simply changed characters. We don't know yet. All we know is that she cried a lot, and we did, too. She told us she missed us, and we told her the same. She laughed some, as well, and she told us a little about her drug. "You would love it," she told Grant, and her voice held such a note of longing right then that I became immensely sad. *She was longing for company,* I thought. *She was longing for a friend to follow her.*

We took her to a treatment center, where they were expecting her, and that is where it ended that day. Though where it will end altogether is still unknown.

That is just the way it is. You crawl through garbage to get to a toilet, but you gotta keep going, because past that there is a light. Some friends will follow you and some won't, even if you're already there to tell them the coast is clear. All you can do is call to them, begging from the other side.

Friends & Lovers

An Unsuccessful Intervention

IT'S A GIVEN THAT GRANT IS BAD AT ABDUCTING PEOPLE. But I had hope for Lary. You'd think Lary would be the perfect predator, but no. In fact they have both been threatening to kidnap me for weeks now, but when it comes to a decent intervention, I have to say they're both about as useful as a big bag of brain tumors. It doesn't help, either, that they each love alcohol, because everyone knows you can't capture anything worth crap when you've been drinking.

"You asstards," I griped into Grant's voicemail. "I've been following my normal routine—I'm standing out in the open right now—and nothing! What the hell kind of incompetent, booger-eating kidnappers are you?"

"Bitch," Grant snipped when he called me back, "don't push me. This is an emergency. Something needs to be done."

So we all met for breakfast later that morning. "Just what the hell am I doing that's so bad, anyway?" I asked, because—and maybe this says something—I didn't think to ask until then.

"What do you mean, what the hell are you doing?" Lary asked, incredulous. "Hollis, it's like I don't even know you. When was the last time you got drunk? When was the last time you flashed your tits at a tiki bar and went home with the waiter? God, it's like you've been replaced by a pod from Planet Pussy! Who *are* you?"

"It's true," Grant added gravely. "You're upholding your responsibilities and conducting yourself in a civilized manner. A lot of people are really worried about you."

"Jesus God!" I huffed. "Have you guys ever met me? I stopped drinking two years ago. Two years! And you just now noticed?"

Here these two reptiles claim to be my best friends, yet they had all this time to intervene—all these chances—and didn't take a single one. Instead they just allowed me to slip into sobriety. What's worse is that I didn't even know my last drink was my last. I just remember thinking I'd cut back on alcohol a bit, then that whittled down to nothing, and now two years later I'm still thinking I'll get back around to it one of these days, but stuff keeps coming up.

Because drinking, if you're gonna do it right, takes a lot of time and commitment. I know because I used to be really good at it. Much better than Grant, for example, who still conducts a neighborhood tour of all the vomit markings he made the night he famously chased his three-day lemon-juice "cleanse" with two pitchers of Bazooka martinis. But that was then. Now, like I said, things keep coming up, and all of a sudden I like looking around me without booze blurring the view.

Take the time, in this very diner, when my girl burst into an impromptu display of interpretive dancing right along the linoleum. It was sudden and fleeting and unplanned—and even kind of awkward, because people were eating and stuff, but thankfully no one interrupted her, and she twirled and shimmied and waved her arms with absolute certainty of her abilities. I remember thinking this was the beginning of a slew of future episodes exactly like this. Really, I thought there would be tons more chances to catch her as a three-year-old performing with such gusto and seriousness, but years have

Friends & Lovers

passed and it turns out that was my only chance. That was it. *Pffftt.* Gone.

Thank God I caught it. What if I'd been drinking and that moment simply fell into the puddle of other booze-muddled memories living in the periphery of my brain? But it isn't. I captured it. I have it now to take out and admire like a tiny trophy. And even though that moment has come and gone, there's a constant litany of others that prattle by so rapidly they're like pebbles in the palm of a Kung Fu master, and I'm the apprentice charged with plucking them up before they're whisked away. I feel like I have to be alert to keep them from escaping. That's why I don't drink, because everyone knows you can't capture anything worth crap when you've been drinking.

Grant eyed me keenly. "We need to take action," he said, and Lary nodded.

"You bunch of bottom-fish," I told them, "you're too late."

Stay on the Bike

WHEN I HEARD THAT DANIEL GOT A JOB CAT-SITTING, I thought, Jesus God, don't these people check references? We're talking about a guy who killed his last pets in cold blood. Granted, they were goldfish, but still. He had named them Ruby and Pearl.

"Did you tell them you ruthlessly murdered your own pets?" I asked.

"That was an accident," Daniel insisted.

"How do you 'accidentally' grind up your goldfish in the garbage disposal?" I asked.

And don't even get me started about Mitch's obese cat, Jenny. When Daniel and Mitch first made plans to move in together, Daniel kept suggesting that Jenny could live just fine fifteen miles away in a monthly storage compartment in Doraville. "Just leave an open bag of food on the floor and she'll be okay," he said.

But since then Daniel has turned all cat-crazy, and now he's madly in love with Jenny. He even sends out mass e-mails at regular intervals called "Jenny's Quote of the Week," accompanied by jpegs of Jenny lounging in the sea of her own feline blubber, like a furry Buddha dispensing pearls of wisdom. "If only man can but love one another, the world will be at peace," Jenny will say, or something of similar depth and insight. Grant cannot wait to get Jenny's quotes; he'll walk around all morning afterward, talking in Jenny-speak. "If only man can but wipe his ass, the world will be less shitty," or something of similar depth and insight.

"Leave Jenny alone, you crusty old claw hammer," I'll say to him. "Man needs to but love each other, for fuck's sake!" I'll laugh. Because you have to laugh. In the ocean of crap that comes at you every day through e-mail and other avenues, the occasional little pedantic acumen coming from a cat can't be that bad. We're all stuck here in the same flaming ball of bitterness the world has become; we're all inundated to the point of paralysis by a daily tsunami of over-information. Any little missive that isn't hate-filled or downright heartbreaking is a gem, I figure, and it should be treasured.

"If Hollis can but get laid," Grant will pontificate grandly, "the world would be at peace."

The other day at The Local, where Grant bartends, a customer complained to Grant about Jenny's Quotes. Evidently he'd somehow gotten on Daniel's mailing list and was now the unwilling recipient of Jenny's wisdom. The conversation matriculated and pretty soon most of the bar was talking in Jenny-speak.

"If only man can but get a goddamn beer, the world wouldn't have to die of thirst right here in front of the bartender."

"If only man can but shut the fuck up, the bartender wouldn't have to throw the world out on its ass."

Pretty soon everybody was celebrating another day of relative comfort, eased into the mind-set by a rotund cat and her quote of the week. The whole thing reminded me of a bike race I rode once when I was in my early twenties. The course was seventy-five miles over Mexican terrain from Tecate to Endenada, with a nine-mile mountain smack in the middle. Everybody warned me about the incline, and I have to admit I was in over my head. The trick, I was told, was not to get off your bike. "Whatever you do," all my sage bike-rider friends told me, "don't get off and walk. You lose all your momentum. Stay on your bike no matter how slow you have to pedal."

It's ironic that, by race day, all these same bike-rider friends flaked for various reasons and I ended up doing the race alone, and when I hit that incline, believe me, it was every molecule as miserable as they told me it would be. I was about to get off my bike to walk, because tons of others were doing it and I sincerely believed my tongue was about to get caught in my spokes, when I heard another rider behind me say, "No, you don't."

"Huh?" I grunted, hot and wretched.

"Stay on or you'll never make it," he said. "So where are you from? I'm from El Centro . . . right around the corner here there'll be a support station, you can stop there . . . I graduated from San Diego State, and you? . . . Oops, it must be the next corner, oh well, keep pedaling . . . So tell me about yourself, been riding long? . . . My mistake, it must be the next corner. I swear you can stop there . . . "

And on he went, this irritating voice that seemed as endless as the hill I was climbing until, before I knew it, I was at the top and the struggle was over. And that's how I feel about Jenny's Quotes. Times are tough, we're on a hill, and we keep turning corners only to see there's more of a hill. But one day—I swear—one day we'll turn a corner to see the hill has crested. That's why Jenny's Quotes are important. They're not an irksome interruption. They're not! They're little rubies and pearls, distracting us from our own misery so we can make it to the next corner. If only these people could grasp that. If only they could give Jenny a little appreciation. If only man can but stay on the bike, the world will be at peace.

Friends & Lovers

Daniel's Hands

At first I thought it was a good thing Daniel finally got a professional haircut, because otherwise I didn't see who'd hire his skinny ass, what with his hair looking like it's been attacked by bats. But he's been applying at a lot of coffeehouses lately, where the employers seem to command a shocking appearance from their workers. Christian, a barista at a coffeehouse down the street from me, has his black hair chopped in cantilevered layers with patches dyed alternately cloud white or cobalt blue or both, depending on his mood, and I must say I like looking at him.

"Muss it up a little," I tell Daniel, but he swats my hand away from his head. We are on the patio of the new Caribou in the just-built Target shopping center that all the in-town people were cursing until it came time to buy a shower curtain; now nobody can live without the place. Daniel's medication is working and his condition is stabilized to the point where he seems healthier than any of us these days, and now he's insistent he work at a corporate coffeehouse because he wants to be buried in "holdings," whatever those are.

"Benefits, bitch," he explains. "Health, dental, stock options. At Starbucks, they give you a benefits package just for working part time," he slams the tabletop for emphasis. "Part time."

Daniel has never worked a corporate job his whole life, unless you count that short-lived gig at The Gap eight million years ago, which coincides with the period during which they folded all their inventory into anal triangles. Now I know why. Daniel is about as fastidious as they come, barring his hair. Keiger regularly insists that of the two of us, Daniel is the only one he'd consider actually hiring, which I really resent, but still I asked Keiger to make good on that. Unfortunately I'm still heavily in debt to him for rehiring Grant after Grant made his grand, heralded, ticker-tape exit that year and then all of a sudden needed his job back. So Daniel's on his own except for my help, which is dubious.

"Don't work at Starbucks," I whine. "My brother worked there and they sucked the life out of him." It's true. My brother was placed as a manager of a Starbucks in Compton, California, which was the equivalent to hiring a Quaker to helm a strip club. My brother did it for the benefits package, too, left his job parking cars in the paradise of Lake Tahoe so he could clock in at five a.m. and be accused of discrimination for insisting his subordinates clock in on time as well. After years of being overlooked for obvious promotions, but hanging on anyway, for the benefits, he was finally fired due to some offense manufactured by those former underlings.

The last job Daniel had, a six-year stint as an instructor at the same privately owned mental-health facility for emotionally damaged children where Grant used to work, made certain to dump his ass within days of his becoming eligible for said pot-of-gold benefits package, if I recall. So now Daniel is looking to be a cog in the quagmire, just one gerbil among thousands on a big wheel where the bigwigs are too busy making money to discriminate when one of them is getting close to crossing over into the tenured territory of the "benefits-worthy." But there's a cost. There really is.

Friends & Lovers

"Hollis, I don't have a choice. I've worked all my life, and look at me," he splays his arms toward me across the table. "My hands are empty."

I wish I could answer that, but the truth is I'm hardly in a position to talk. For years I've been balancing on the line that is supposed to separate the sanctuary of a corporate job from the uncertain abyss of entrepreneurism. It looks mighty similar on both sides of the fence, so if you have to jump, you might as well do so on the side that lets you dictate your own time. My brother is now an entrepreneur, which I have no idea what that means in his case, except to say that when he's a hundred years old and empty-handed, at least his hands will be empty because he'd personally used up what could have been in them, rather than having tossed it all fresh and lovely at the feet of a corporation in exchange for the nebulous promise of future security.

I look at Daniel's hands, which literally are the hands of an artist, and I'm pained and selfish in my regret that they'll be doing anything other than creating more beautiful pieces like those of his that hang in local art galleries—warm and lovely work with an amazing depth that took years and years to perfect. Daniel's hands are still on the table, outstretched, so I put mine in his and squeeze. "Your hands," I say, "are not empty."

The Wreckage of Joan Collins

I SUPPOSE IT'S SAYING SOMETHING THAT GRANT did not die, though technically it could still happen. It's true that he presently seems to be up and walking around in a kind of quasi-state of okay-ness, but he could still have one of those freak neck fractures or something, like in the urban myth when that guy walked around seemingly fine after a fender bender, then six days later someone slapped him on the back hello and he dropped down dead on the spot. So I have been slapping Grant on the back plenty since his car accident last week, but so far nothing.

"Ouch," he'd say. "Stop that."

"You pussy," I taunted him.

He did complain about a general stiffness, though, which I guess is to be expected after you've called all your friends to tell them you went through the windshield of your car; Not that Grant went through the windshield of his car, it's just that he called and told everybody he did. "And my car is totaled," he groaned over the phone.

This, of course, I had to see. He'd wrecked it right at the corner of North Highland and Greenwood Avenues, one of the most visible intersections in the world. Nine years ago, I got blotto drunk at that intersection while waiting for the Olympic torch relay to finally go by, and to this day I still encounter people who recognize me as the fool who thought it would be fun to crawl on the hood of the lead car as it tried to inch its way through the crowd. In my mind I lay there all sexy, like Michelle Pfeiffer on the piano in *The Fabulous Baker Boys*, but in reality, as it has been recounted to me over the years, I was simply sprawled awkwardly on the grill like a dead moose. So I find it fitting that Grant suffered public humiliation in the same place.

Even before the car wreck, it was becoming a consensus that this particular car brought out the bad in Grant. He has owned about nineteen cars since I met him, some for even less than the mere six weeks he'd had this one, but none of them caused him to careen down side streets like a crazed Iraqi tank like this one did. It was a white, turbo-charged 1986 convertible Chrysler Le Baron, with leather interior the color of ox blood and a body so metal-heavy you could melt it down to make a collection of oil barges. He christened it "Joan Collins," and in six weeks he'd been ticketed twice, and that's not even counting the time we were pulled over on our way to sneak into the Inman Park Parade last month. That officer, who we believe was the notorious six-foot-four transsexual police woman of the Old Fourth Ward, simply listened to his pleadings ("Seriously, I used to be a deacon"), gave him a look that could have curdled the earth's core, and let us go on our way. It might have mattered that Grant was not speeding in that particular instance, or even driving, but rather he was perched with his ass on the back headrest as he bellowed through a bullhorn, "Lies, lies, it's all lies!"

Later, after Grant told me of the accident and its aftermath, I had the choice of first going to see him or see the wreckage of *Joan Collins,* so of course I chose the latter. He'd made the accident sound like a scene straight out of *Hollywood Babylon,* with blood and twisted shrapnel mixed with bits of Jayne Mansfield's brains splattered on the asphalt along with a little dead Chihuahua and an empty-yet-perfectly-intact whiskey bottle. Who could resist that? Yet when I arrived there was barely any evidence of a disaster. The crowd had dispersed, and *Joan Collins* had been pushed to a metered parking space and looked to have suffered a couple of drastic collapses of the steering wheel and bumper variety. Oh, and there was a crack in her windshield. "Bitch," I yelled at Grant as I approached him soon afterward, "when you tell me you totaled your car and went through the windshield, I wanna see some carnage! Look at you, you do not even have any blood in your hair!" Then I slapped him on the back.

He was recuperating not in a hospital but on the patio of The Local, where he actually expected to bartend that night. "He looks terrible," I told Keiger. And he did. Car crashes take a lot out of you, even if you don't leave any of your brains or blood behind. Plus Grant kept clutching his big barrel chest, which had been what slammed against Joan's steering wheel and caused it to collapse. Lary had been duly alerted and was on the way with a supply of pirated painkillers, but in the meantime Grant looked like a wreck himself, so I slapped him on the back again.

"Ouch, stop that."

"You pussy," I said again, and we laughed a little, me and Grant, with my hand on his back and his hand on his chest. Seeing us like that, you would have thought I was looking down at Grant's big head right then and being damn happy he didn't have blood in his hair. You would have sworn I was thanking sweet Jesus that he had walked away, however stiffly, from the wreckage of *Joan Collins*.

Friends & Lovers

Inventing the Rules

<hr>

DANIEL, WHO IS NORMALLY NOBLE, COULDN'T STOP laughing when I told him I actually attend all the requisite seminars at the Department of Labor in order to receive my weekly unemployment checks. "Isn't that the rule?" I asked.

"You loser," Daniel laughed, "you're supposed to charm your way past that."

Me? Charm? My first day there I got in a fight with the security guard, but who can blame me? He makes you stand in line when there is no line. In fact, there is no reason for him to be there at all, as everyone there is as docile as diseased livestock. It's not like there's actual money back there in those cubicles we can steal, though there are staplers and stuff. I could actually use another stapler. But as it was, I was just using one of the computers in the big bank of computers they have there for us to use, or so one would think.

"Young lady, you can't use that computer," the security guard told me, and whenever people tell me I can't do something I usually take it as a polite suggestion, because in my book polite suggestions can be politely declined. "Thank you, officer," I said, "but I don't need your help, because as you can see I am perfectly capable of using this computer."

"No, you need to stand in line. All those people are before you," he said, pointing to an area that was, as far as I could tell, completely empty, as were all the other computers.

"What people?" I asked, looking around. The place is bigger than an airplane hangar.

"Those people," he said, and he waved his arm to indicate that, in the distance, there were some tiny antlike people barely perceptible on the earth's curve, people who not only were nowhere near us but were not even in line. They were milling around in a whole other part of the horizon in a different time zone.

"You're kidding," I said, and he gave me the look that security guards have to remind people they've got a gun and they're not afraid to invent reasons to use it, which made me pause.

Because right then I was reminded of a guy I met on the island in Greece way back when being jobless was a joke and no big deal. I'd been hanging there for weeks, funding my beer intake by beating people at pool at a place called Zanzibar, where the owner, a mean-hearted round man named Marco, charged backpackers one dollar to take a cold shower from an open hose located a few feet from the cafe tables.

It was a big perk, I tell you, but I couldn't stay there forever. Soon I had to begin the journey home to try for that job as a Xerox copy salesperson (or whatever) that my comparative literature professor told me my degree in writing would get me. Actual writing itself only got me to Greece, where I frolicked with naked Danish backpackers in that shower every day, and I was practically certain there were rules that said you couldn't earn a living doing that. Or I had at least been told there were rules that said that.

The man who owned Zanzibar also had the taxi syndicate under his thumb, so it was necessary to go through him to pre-order a taxi to get you to the port early enough to catch the ferry that morning, as the bus wouldn't arrive in time, he said. That was the rule. Everybody did it. "Otherwise, you'll have to spend the night at the port," Marco said.

But the morning I was to leave, my pre-dawn, pre-ordered, pre-paid, pre-save-my-ass taxi didn't arrive, so I pounded on Marco's door until he called me a "fat brown-cow bitch" and chased me off his property waving a rotten melon. There was nothing for me to do but catch the bus to the port anyway, since I couldn't stay in the village another night, not with Marco and his melon after me. I was worried about how I was going to fend for myself alone overnight at a Greek dock until the bus pulled into the port and there was the ferry sitting there as patiently as a big basset hound, not scheduled to leave for a few hours yet. I couldn't believe my luck until the immigration officer told me the ferry is always scheduled to leave after the bus arrives.

"But Marco told me the rule was to get a taxi," I said.

"Marco," the official laughed, "he invented that rule to make a living."

Now here I was years later looking at this security officer at the unemployment office doing the same thing, inventing rules to make a living. He can't have people using computers willy-nilly, looking up vocations, getting jobs and stuff, now can he? If everyone got jobs, what would happen to his? "Those are the rules," he repeated. So I left. I can invent rules, I thought. I can. For one, that rule about it not being possible to earn a living while frolicking with naked Danish backpackers or any other way I want? My first rule is that that rule is crap.

I Know It When I See It

YOU'D THINK THAT BY MY POPULARITY ALONE, Keiger would offer my unemployed ass a job bartending at The Local. But I guess there are two huge flaws in my argument: One, they don't need another bartender; and two, the reason I'm so popular is because the single time I did bartend there, I gave away all the alcohol. Still, who the hell does he think he is? He hired goddamn Grant to be a bartender when the only bar experience Grant had was sitting on the other side of it demanding they forego the glasses and just pour the hooch directly into that Grand Canyon he calls a mouth. And yet I—who was practically raised in a bar—couldn't even score a side shift as, say, a busboy or something.

"No way in hell," Keiger laughs, adding that he is so seriously not even ever gonna hire me as a bartender that I should immediately start looking elsewhere for a fallback career. "You should write your book," he says.

Keiger has been using that as an excuse not to hire me for years, and I cannot tell you how mad that makes me. I remember when Keiger first offered Grant a job years ago. We—me, Grant, Lary, and Daniel—had been hanging out there since the place opened. Keiger honed in on our foursome, plucked Grant up like a truffle in a pig trough, put him behind the bar, and taught him everything he knew. Then he simply let Grant radiate his Grant vibes, and before you knew it that place was packed like a frat-house phone booth. Lary loved it,

Friends & Lovers

because Lary could go there every night that Grant worked and just sit there like the goddamn barnacle that he is, with his tongue rolled out over the top of the bar. Personally, though, this development made me stew. It didn't help that after I had Milly, Grant told me Keiger didn't like me bringing her there.

"I can't believe I'm being discriminated against," I had bitched to Grant. I had brought one of those baby seats that hook onto the edge of things and serve as a suspended appendage of sorts, a kind of auxiliary pod for Milly to sit in while she played with her big, multicolored plastic caterpillar on the bar top. I was really good about only having Milly's diaper bag spread out over the surface that was right in front of me, plus maybe, I swear just a molecule, a little bit overlapping onto the garnish tray. But it was early and we were the only customers in there, anyway. And I wasn't even ordering anything, so what's the big goddamn deal?

"Get out, bitch," Grant said to me, his face close. It was then that I realized it was *Grant,* not Keiger, who didn't want Milly and me there. And I remembered that this was the second time a bartender had tried to throw me out of a bar.

The first was when I was seven. Kitty, my father's favorite bartender at the Thin Lizzy, got all upset one night. I guess she had issues of her own and it didn't help that she was really popular so her customers always bought her shots—my dad foremost among them.

Anyway, that night Kitty had stayed after her shift to party with her patrons; even my mother came to join in. There we were, my sisters and I, being jostled about between well-meaning drunk people, when Kitty took me aside and told me to get out. "Get out," she implored. "This is no place for you." I think she got it into her head that I wouldn't ever make my way past where we were right then, and she was adamant that this place was no good for me. I was only seven and liked that place fine, but her words have resonated with me ever since.

Keiger makes sure to remind me of the days when we first met, years ago when I used to sit on his balcony writing story after story in my notebooks. "You're a writer," he says. "You should write for a living."

He's the most begrudging with compliments, so it made me think maybe I could pull it off. I sent some pieces to editors and amazingly landed a column in a small paper based on nothing but my reliable moray-eel of a personality. Still, though, I need real income.

"It's because you care so much about me, isn't it?" I tell Keiger. "That's why you won't hire me."

"Seriously," he replies. "You are the worst bartender." And then he hugs me. It's a real hug; he pulls me into the nape of his neck as if I fit there like a fuzzy muffler.

"But they love me," I whimper.

"I'd love you, too, if you gave me my booze for free," Keiger says.

But if you ask me, there are two huge flaws in his argument: One, he doesn't drink; and two, he already loves me. Maybe it's not the treat-her-like-a-queen kinda love, but still. Love is love. I know it when I see it.

Friends & Lovers

Question Mark

LARY SAYS HE'S GONNA WAIT UNTIL HE'S SIXTY before he sucks his first cock, which I think is ridiculous. "Why wait?" I ask. "What if it turns out you like it?"

"Exactly," he counters. "I figure if I like it I'll have little time left to do it."

I personally would never trust anything tender between this man's teeth, but that doesn't mean he should wait until he's sixty to be gay if that's what he is. Lary's gayness has always been a big question mark between Grant and me. Grant is certain Lary's gay and he just hasn't had the right amount of tequila to admit it. Me, I've known Lary longer than Grant and I'm convinced otherwise. At best, Lary's sexuality remains a question mark. "Gay is relative," he says, and certain question marks are simply worth keeping.

But hell, who knows what any of us will be at any time in our lives? I remember back in college when I'd somehow convinced myself I was a straight-A student, and damn if my GPA didn't reflect this belief right up until I graduated. I'm talking about the degree I got after I flunked out during my first foray into college, after deciding to start over at another university.

I got the idea after going to Hawaii with what was left of my family after my dad died. My mother got it into her head that we'd better start doing stuff together as a family while we were all within reasonable distance of each other. My brother at the time lived in a beach town up the coast, where he shared an apartment with a mob of horny grad students. He himself worked as a waiter at a steak restaurant, but he was in his eighth year at Long Beach State and would graduate eventually. I don't judge. Counting the two years I squandered before I started over, it took me six years to get my degree.

But back to Hawaii; we got the condo in Makaha through my sister Cheryl's connections. She was waiting tables as well at the time, at that restaurant staffed by leggy dames wearing skirts shorter than the aprons around their waists and stiletto heels so high you could hold them to hunt bison. It was the closest thing to a Playboy Club we had in San Diego, and most of the patrons were rich guys with flared collars and pinky rings. One of them owned the condo and gave the key to Cheryl so we could use it for a week. It was located next to a massive Sheraton resort property, and that first night I got blotto on mai tais, stole a golf cart, and crashed it into an irrigation ditch. Fun times.

The next morning I lay around at the condo, the one owned by the rich guy, too hung over from my copious underage drinking to go with the rest of my family to the Hawaiian culture center, where I hear a bunch of big-bellied men with tattooed faces roasted a pig and served it with poi. The condo was furnished like a corporate hotel suite, with no evidence of a personal residence at all except a collection of books on a shelf in the bedroom, one of which was *The Lazy Man's Way to Riches* by Richard Gilly Nixon.

Hell, I thought, *I like riches, and I damn well know I'm lazy,* as I'd been told I was lazy all my life. I remember as a child eavesdropping on my parents as they joked about the future employment prospects of each of their offspring, and when they got to me, my mother pondered, "What will Hollis become?" and my father, without missing a beat, laughed, "Fired!" So I pocketed Nixon's book and carried it to the beach.

I read half the book, up until the part where it started to get specific about the path to riches, which involved mail-order of some kind. I did read the part that heralded goal setting and warned of the energy-draining effects of masturbation on the brains of young achievers. "Read your goals every night before you go to bed, and every morning when you wake up."

So I made a list and kept it under my pillow, unfolding it every night and every morning. I wish I still had the list, because it would be fun to see if, all these years later, any of the goals listed so long ago match my actual accomplishments. Here are a few I remember: I want to be a straight-A student. Check. I want to own my own home. Check. I want to be a published writer. Check. I want to be rich. Question mark.

The list was very long, believe me, and I read it every morning and every night for exactly five months until I fell in love with a bartender and commenced having all the energy-sapping orgasms the book had warned about. But I still marvel at how just five months of resolute goal setting did seem to set a direction for me that led me to the life I now have, one with more checks and less question marks. I used to wonder what I would have accomplished had I just kept it up and forsaken all the side trails, but not any longer. Riches are relative, I say, and certain question marks are simply worth keeping.

Nude Naked Women

LARY IS POUTING, WHICH I DIDN'T THINK was possible. I had no idea
he had that in his limited repertoire of expressions. I've known him a
long time, and as far as I could tell, he had two gears: evil and quietly
evil. Take the time he helped me move after I left fifty phone messages threatening to contact his stalker—the one with the fake tits big
enough to be seen from other solar systems—to tell her he didn't die
horribly in a mining accident after all. "Pick up the phone, ass-tard,"
I hollered into his voicemail, "or little Miss Psycho will be sleeping in
your driveway again."

Lary did not pick up the phone, but he showed up at my house
later that day chipper as a Christian at summer camp. It wasn't until a
month later, when I finally got around to unpacking, that I saw he'd
demolished anything breakable in every box he'd carried. "You didn't
need that shit anyway," was his excuse, and the only reason he's still
my friend is because he's probably right.

And now he is pouting because, he said, I keep misrepresent-
ing his new business venture, the mail-order mosquito-larvae empire.
"They're not mosquito larvae," he keeps insisting. "Don't call them
mosquito larvae."

"But that's exactly what they are. You scooped them out of a
puddle in your carport, for chrissakes," I said. "What the hell else
should I call them?"

"Swamp Buddies."

"Swamp Buddies?" I choked.

Friends & Lovers

"Swamp Buddies, bitch," he said. "It's all in the advertising. Use your imagination."

Jesus God, it's sewer sludge. I don't care how you package it, who the hell is gonna fork over dough for diseased vector eggs? Of course, I remember when I was a kid I sent off for a packet of magic Sea Monkeys. The packet was probably no more than a few pellets of compressed anthrax, but still, after I added the water, I fully expected the sludge to evolve into the enchanted population of regal little creatures depicted in the comic-book ad, including the smiling Sea Monkey King complete with crown and triton. I planned to name him Ferdinand, stage assassinations, and enact tiny little world wars.

But all I got was a festering little splooge of silt, which did little to inspire my imagination. Maybe my little sister with the toy monkey that picked her daisies and cheated at cards, maybe *she* would have seen the king with his crown and triton, and the rest of the royalty ruling over a divided class of plebes and merchants. But not me. Thank gawd my mother flushed it before it could solidify and terrorize the town.

You'd think I'd learn my lesson after that, but I am a volcanic sucker when it comes to advertising. Later, as a dumb teenager, I succumbed to a flyer I found at the liquor store next to the bar where my father spent his days, and I sent away for a picture that promised, for 50 cents, the pornographic depiction of a "nude naked" woman having sex with a turtle. All I can say in my defense was that there were no offers of other pornographic pictures, because if there were other options—like for pictures of nude naked women having sex with nude naked men—then maybe I would have picked those. But my only choice was girl-on-turtle, so I had to go with that.

I filled out the flyer, taped two quarters to it, and mailed it off. Believe it or not, I actually received a picture in the mail. It was of a jowly, rheumy-eyed bag lady lying on a sidewalk with a turtle on her stomach. She wasn't naked, and the turtle was plastic. But by that time the nude-naked people had my two quarters and what was I supposed to do? I had to take my lumps and toss the photo.

I found it a year later tucked into the stack of jack-off mags my brother kept stuffed under his desk. Looking back, it was quite a vanilla variety of porn, and all the girls had those '70s super muffs that require a machete to clear a path. I thoroughly examined each photo, and in the end I could not imagine how this ratty pack of grainy, angle-challenged amateur shots could excite anyone, but it was not *my* imagination that mattered in this regard.

You see, in my own room, I had my own stack of magazines packed with pictures of toothy teen idols. I played sappy ballads and envisioned the exchange of tender affections. I enacted courtships, betrayals, and passionate reconciliations. I fainted into imaginary arms. Over and over, I was completely entranced by the packaging.

Normally this memory would unleash an assload of smarmy self-loathing, but I'm weary lately, weighted with the realization that you do what you can with the ingredients you get. You add water. You hope something will grow. You wait and anticipate and pine. In the end, you either get magic or you get another puddle of sewer sludge.

It all depends on your imagination.

Friends & Lovers

185

A Pussy-Ass Princess

I REALLY DIDN'T FEEL LIKE GETTING NAKED IN FRONT of Grant, especially if it was just for the sake of garnering some sympathy. "I swear, I'm covered in bruises," I told him. "Just trust me."

"Like hell, you pussy-ass bitch," he bitched at me. He was still mad at me for making him worry last week, when I fell twenty feet off a ladder and landed on my face. I should have called someone to help me, he insisted.

"Like you pussies are ever any help," I tried to laugh, but all of a sudden I *felt like crying*. I didn't even cry when I had the accident, but now I just wanted to sit down and jibber. And it was not the pain—I can handle pain—it was that Grant was right, I should have called someone. I should have called Keiger, but I am terrified to need him these days, even though I know he loves me. Sure it's a tolerate-her-like-a-hemorrhoid kinda love, but I know love when I see it.

And that's saying something considering that, at fourteen, I read a truckload of my mother's epic romance novels. I would seriously recommend against that. Epic romances are really just she-porn, in which the heroine gets gang-raped, thrown in jail, and dragged behind a horse, all by the guy she loves, who couldn't help himself on account of how he had been driven wild with an accidental glimpse of the small of her back.

Somehow, though, epic romance writers make it all seem so desirable to a fourteen-year-old whose hormone-addled romance lobe is still forming. The first one I read involved an incandescently beautiful peasant girl as the object of desire for two rival monarchs whose crotches explode every time they gaze upon her visage. These men show their passion by torturing and degrading her for four hundred pages, but in the end all her suffering pays off when she gets to ride off and live horribly ever after with the man who treated her the crappiest.

In short, those books fucked me up. I seriously spent decades, it seemed like, just lying in languid silhouette of the setting sun in hopes someone would want to long for me. That was a major waste of time. All I ended up with was a boyfriend who broke up with me by pushing me out of his car. Granted, it was a VW, and granted, it was parked at the time, and granted, I was clinging to him like a lovesick jellyfish and there really was no other way to get my bawling, begging ass out the door, but still. He moved to Australia, like, the next day, so frantic he was to escape the tendrils of my epic-romance-tainted expectations.

I have since become a jaded, misanthropic, smirk-prone hermit crab, which I swear to God (probably) is a more realistic stance to take when tackling life. I don't really have any expectations. Take the last time Keiger took me on a date. Fifteen minutes after the movie started, he got up to get more popcorn and, uh, never came back. It didn't help, I guess, that I have a habit of yelling at the movie screen. This is especially true when it's playing a romantic comedy. "Ha! Like that's ever gonna happen!" or "Oh, I am so sure!" and such. You can't always get away with that at a movie theater, and the ushers are not always polite when they ask you to leave, either. Anyway, at least Keiger doesn't drag me behind a horse. That's pretty much my criteria for boyfriends these days.

Friends & Lovers

Last week I finally gave in and agreed to read Milly "Rumpel-stiltskin," that miserable fairy tale in which the miller's daughter is imprisoned by a prince and forced to spin straw into gold "if she valued her life." But I read it only on the condition Milly study the postscript I always include at the end of these awful yarns. "If you're ever trapped in a castle, are you gonna sit there and cry?" I implored. "No. You're not. You're gonna keep your wits and find a way out, right?" I pointed to one of the illustrations. "Look, here, see the creepy little Rumpelstiltskin walking through the door? The door is *open,* and what is she doing? She's *just sitting there.* What are you gonna do? You're gonna kick the creepy little man in the crotch and run past him, right? You're gonna escape, right? And what's the worst mistake she made? She *married the prince,* the same selfish pig who put her in the dungeon in the first place. Don't ever, ever do that!"

For chrissakes, I won't even go into Rapunzel. What a simpering idiot she is, sitting at the top of a turret looking forlornly into the horizon for someone to save her. "You're gonna cut off your own damn hair and climb your own damn self down, right?" I tell my girl. Her response, usually, is to roll her eyes like they're loose in her skull.

She's right; I can be high up there with my indignation over the prince-coming-to-get-me concept, then something happens like the day Milly decided she wanted to open a lemonade stand. Her sign itself was awesomely flawed. LEMOADE, it read in raspberry candy stripe, with crude little lemon-slice finials dancing in the borders. She hung it across our door and opened up shop, with an upended laundry basket serving as the counter space for her wares. She had arrayed a few stools out front as well, in a nice welcoming pattern, fully expecting to be flocked with customers, which was optimistic considering we lived on the first floor of an old factory with meager walk-by traffic at the time. Regardless, Milly's face was bursting with such eagerness and joy, it practically paralyzed me with anxiety.

You do not know the meaning of angst until your child is on the verge of facing certain disappointment, when the openness with which she welcomes the world is in danger of being slapped away like naughty fingers off a cake plate. You would do anything, I tell you, to stave that off, to create a pocket of air so her trust can survive a little longer in a world normally polluted with snarkiness and guile.

"Keiger, help," I whispered into my cell phone. "Milly opened a lemonade stand in our hallway. Can you please come and be her customer?"

He was there in exactly five minutes, just in time to banish any uncertainty that might have crept into Milly's eyes.

"Boy, I sure am thirsty," he bellowed as he came down the hall.

At that Milly perked up like a kitten at the sound of a can opener. A flurry of other customers came as well, neighbors and other people Keiger had prompted. They sat, asked for refills, and commended her product. I was so relieved. I know the day will come when the world doesn't answer my daughter the way she hopes, and like any parent, I live in dread of the powerlessness I'm bound to feel before her disappointment. But not today. Today my friends rescued me from that. Today my daughter's pride in herself is so pure and beautiful, it's enough to make me sit here and cry like a pussy-ass princess trapped in a castle.

Friends & Lovers

Nothing without Me

JESUS GOD, IF I NEED ANY MORE EVIDENCE—at all—that I am wasting my life, all I have to do is look around at the bunch of bottom-fish I have for friends. Grant, for one, won't even pick me up at the airport when I ask him. No, he was busy hanging a chandelier above his dining room table. Strike that; he was not even the one hanging the chandelier. He got our neighbor Chris, a lighting designer—not a handyman or a custodian, but a famous designer-artist with a gallery and everything—to hang it, and it wasn't even one of Chris's own creations. It was just some retro-metal number Grant bought retail. So getting this man to install it was like asking Picasso to paint the bathroom, if you ask me, and certainly no goddamn excuse to leave me stranded at the airport.

"I'm his hand-me-this bitch, bitch," Grant bitched back at me.

"Shut up and get your worthless pansy ass to the airport and pick me up!" I shrieked, but by that time Chris was already standing on Grant's table, which, knowing Grant, was probably the whole point. "Stop pretending you have a life without me," I said into the empty line. "You'd be nothing without me, you hear that?"

Next I called Lary, which of course was a whole other mindfuck in futility. He was working. Again. Lary. "Oh, my God! I can't believe you're working again," I wailed. He works all the time now, thus seriously endangering his carefully cultivated image as a burdensome sack of maggots. "You're not supposed to have responsibilities, you retard," I reminded him. "You're supposed to slide through life by masterminding crimes and stuff! Now come get me anyway! They won't miss you for the next hour or so." Lary makes his living rigging things, and unfortunately he was, right then, dangling from a carabiner way high up above stuff and couldn't comfortably extricate himself.

"You douche!" I hollered. "You're nothing without me, got that? Nothing!" Lary, dangling, just laughed, and I could hear the high-uppityness in his voice as he told me to fuck off.

I would have called Daniel, but he is the one who drove me to the airport to begin with, and you don't want to double-impose on people. He'd left a message earlier, to say his mother had called to tell him his father was in the garden shooting armadillos. I really wanted to hear about all the dead armadillos, too, like, can you keep their shells to make lampshades or something, and why does his dad have to shoot them? Can't he just shoo them? But asking a person to make more than one airport run a week is crossing the line. Thank God for Daniel, though.

"I'd be nothing without you," I tell him.

Next I would have called my boyfriend. But I am putting a lot of effort into appearing needless now that I'm unemployed and I don't want to scare Keiger off. The result of that effort is dubious considering the last time I saw him was weeks ago when I had him over for homemade lasagna, which admittedly was a mistake. First of all, Keiger is a really good cook himself. He can make excellent Thai Panang curry with nothing for utensils except an empty tuna can, a crack lighter, and a fondue fork, practically. So I don't know what I was thinking with the lasagna offering except to say that I usually make fabulous lasagna. But my original recipe calls for all kinds of expensive ingredients you get at Whole Foods, like red peppers roasted over a fire of burning gold bullion, sausage made from cows raised on caviar, and cheese aged in bank vaults surrounded by diamonds. In all, one panload of this stuff costs more than a dinner in Paris, plane ticket and all.

Anyway, lately, what with the airline I work for being bankrupt and all, I've been experiencing what I like to call "income limbo," and I can't afford Whole Foods anymore unless it's to go there and troll for food samples, so I've been selecting all my food from the aisle of discounted canned products at Family Dollar. I thought I was being quite resourceful, but in truth I guess my improvised lasagna came out tasting like a plate of solid waste.

That was a few weeks ago, and I know it was bad lasagna, but I didn't think it was disastrous, relationship-wrecking bad. I mean, c'mon. I've known this guy for a long time; he's seen the worst of me, hasn't he? Let's not forget this man has seen me, you know, naked and stuff.

Believe me, when you're naked, there are all kinds of opportunities for unflattering angles. There is just nothing to hide behind. Nothing, and I kind of hate that. Damn, I keep kicking myself, I should not have made the lasagna. Or maybe I should not have let him see me naked. Or maybe it was something else. There must be a million things wrong with me, a trillion. In fact, I am probably just a walking waxball of wrongness, the biggest bottom-fish in the trough. Why else would someone you love leave quietly one night and never call you again? Not a single word. Nada. Nothing.

Lary's New Drug

LARY'S FORMER FAVORITE PASTIME WAS TAKING ACID and climbing scaffolding—not separately, but both together—and notice I said *former.* This is a guy who called me from jail because he threw a metal wrench at a police car from the top of the old Omni Stadium in Atlanta—and he hit the police car! From a block away! All the cops had to do to bust him was simply follow the gazes of admiration coming from the bystanders below.

"I should have thought a little further ahead on that one," he admits. In the end it worked out, though, because while in jail he met a guy who was in for gunrunning, and struck up a friendship that lasted an entire decade before that man disappeared, leaving nothing behind but an old convertible Fiat with the engine running and a tattered Hawaiian shirt in the backseat, or so Lary says.

But let me dispel any notion that I always come to Lary's rescue. That time in jail? He was just calling me to brag, not to make his bail. And the time that Tijuana hooker led him by the hand down a dark alleyway? I was more worried about her (if it *was* a her) than him. In fact, Lary has never needed any of us for anything except possible fodder for amusement. But make no mistake—the day will come when he needs us.

In the meantime, I'm questioning his usefulness. "Goddammit, what the hell good is Lary these days?" I gripe to Grant. "Seriously, don't you think it's time we break into his house again? He's got something in there that's keeping him occupied. We need to see what it is. What if he really did take up taxidermy again like he keeps threatening? We need to check out his basement. He probably has a population of dead hobos down there, all splayed out and polyure-thaned like those poor Chinese corpses in the Bodies exhibit down-town. . . . Oh, my Jesus God! That's gotta be it!" I continued excitedly. "We hardly ever see Lary since that exhibit came to town."

In fact, there used to be a funeral home next to Lary's house until the funeral home got torn down to make room for a cookie-cutter loft complex. I always thought Lary maintained an odd friendship with that undertaker. One night, an agitated mourner set fire to a corpse as it lay in the coffin, and Lary and the undertaker hooted about it after-ward like two neighborhood hens gossiping over the fence. I tell you, it would not surprise me at all if Lary had picked up a few insider secrets and started an amateur undertaking trade all on his own.

When I suggested breaking into Lary's house again to unearth his secret, Grant's interest was piqued. The last time we broke into Lary's place, it was because we had to save him from his alleged meth addiction. We didn't find any meth, or any drugs of any kind—that we recognized, anyway—and we certainly didn't find Lary strung out on the floor, but what we did find was his place in a very orderly condition, which confirmed our suspicions that Lary was on some new drug. We don't know what it is—yet—but we'll find it. We will rescue Lary whether he needs it or not. That's what friends are for.

"I think I saw some embalming fluid in the back of his truck the other day," Grant surmised.

"We can be in and out in minutes," I said.

"It's for his own good," Grant rationalized, grabbing his keys.

"Of course," I agreed, "his own good."

Pressure Cooker

GRANT AND I STILL HAVE YET TO BREAK INTO Lary's house, for which I blame Grant, who actually called Lary and told him to expect us. "Jesus God, Lary can't be expecting us!" I shrieked. "Last weekend he just bought his third gun from some guy in a Waffle House parking lot."

"Hollis," Grant said, "that is exactly why I called him."

After some thought I realized Grant is probably right. Lary is a lot less dangerous when he's expecting you. Take Y2K for example. Remember Y2K? Lary was the only person I know who didn't cop to the least bit of freak in anticipation of Y2K. Even I bought into it a bit by hiding an industrial-size can of yams on the bottom shelf of the baker's rack in my kitchen. I know that doesn't sound like a lot, but I am notoriously lazy in the face of any approaching Armageddon, plus I felt like I was a hundred months pregnant at the time.

Anyway, I called Lary on Y2K eve to tell him to expect me in case the world came to an end, because the truth is there's no better preparation for disaster than to be on the list of Lary's friends. He lives in a stone compound, for chrissakes. The only way Grant and I can break in is if we use my key, which Lary gave me ten years ago because of all my failed attempts to break in. In all, those attempts resulted in a half-dozen shattered windows and a minor shower of gunfire (the gunfire, he says, was just because he wasn't expecting me). This is why Grant has the foresight to call Lary in advance whenever we have a hankering to break into his house these days.

Friends & Lovers

"We're coming over, don't stand in our way," I informed Lary, sounding very resolute.

"Nobody's stopping you," Lary shrugged.

He was, after all, sitting right next to me at the Majestic Diner. Grant and I had persuaded him to come meet us by swearing the owner had recently added Wild Turkey to the breakfast menu. We might have been able to pull off the Wild Turkey thing if the actual owner didn't happen to walk in while we were there, which killed my plans to stock some used bottles behind the register. But luckily, Lary didn't detonate like I thought he would; he just sat down and ordered some coffee.

"I keep all my drugs in the pressure cooker," he added. "Help yourself."

Damn him. It's just like Lary to suck all the fun out of an intervention by being open and honest and refusing to skulk around. It takes the excitement out of confiscating all his heroin or huffing glue or whatever the hell his new drug is these days. We're all curious about that; what Lary is consuming lately, or vice versa. He's always telling stories about experimenting with weird-ass prescription crap he brought back from Central America, stuff like Ritalin, antipsychotics, and asthma medication. This is a far cry from the drugs of back in the day when vintage addicts all popped cool-sounding drugs like "bennies" and "black beauties." Lary, for example, will hork anything from Peruvian Xanax to opiated chewing tobacco from Sweden, which he says you can buy at the Nicaraguan duty-free. This comprises his "stash," he says, which he keeps in his pressure cooker, which itself is kept on the dresser next to his bed.

"I don't even know where I got it," Lary says of his pressure cooker, which he's never actually used to cook anything, and I say this knowing certain drugs do take some cooking. "It just showed up one day."

This is no surprise. Lary regularly awakens to find himself surrounded by strange objects, and I'm not just talking about the fake boobs as big as orbiting moons on his second-to-last girlfriend. He woke up once to find a truck on his roof, for example. Things disappear, as well. His cat Mona has been missing for a year and a half.

"So what are you saying? Some fairy came in the night while you were sleeping and left you a pressure cooker to keep all your drugs in?" I asked.

He practiced his poker face.

"There's no drugs in your pressure cooker!" I shouted at Lary. "You are a big fat lying sack of maggots! All addicts are liars!"

"Well," he said, taking a gingerly sip of his coffee, "I must not be an addict then."

Control the Hole

LARY DRAWS THE LINE AT HOMICIDE, HE SAYS. Like this is some new development. Like until recently homicide was perfectly inside the line but now he's on an anti-killing kick. "It's been a week," he smiles that evil smile, "and I hardly even feel the urge."

"Don't tell me about your damn urges, you demented old dick sack," I say. Jesus God, we've already been sitting here for the past hour listening to Grant talk about how easy it is to suppress his own urges—mainly his urge to eat like a normal person, as opposed to the caterpillar he thinks he is lately, seeing as how he's on day twenty of a new diet that consists solely of fruit, beans, and rice. All I can say is I sure as hell hope he's wearing an adult diaper, because a diet like that is dangerous, I tell you. It'll percolate in your guts until it blows out the back of your ass like a shotgun blast, and that's not something I want to see.

"I feel fabulous," Grant chirps, placing a slice of dried pineapple on his tongue like it was a Communion wafer.

I tried his diet for one week. It was supposed to clean me out internally, leave me all fresh and feeling energetic, when the fact is I seriously thought I was gonna die horribly clutching my eyes like the victim of a biblical curse. "My head is killing me," I complained to him. "Am I supposed to feel like this? Why does this diet hurt my head?" And where was all the energy Grant said I'd feel? I was more energetic when my diet consisted solely of Slim Jims and chocolate-covered peanuts. Granted, I was eighteen then and could have eaten my own moped and probably felt healthier than I do now, but even so—even today—after a week of peeled grapes and crushed peach seeds, you'd think I'd at least get a spring in my step or something.

"Like I said, I feel fabulous," Grant repeats, smug. "I don't know what your problem is."

That right there is what has me furious lately, because Grant and Lary both constantly gloat over how easy it is for them to control their urges, and we are talking normal urges, like the perfectly normal urge to eat a bowl of brownie batter for breakfast. It's just so easy for them to keep from doing that. Me, though, what the hell else have I got to live for? I don't have any abnormal urges I can amp up in order to suppress the normal ones, like I can't go copulate with twice as many Mexican busboys like Grant does, and I can't taxidermy twenty extra animal corpses in my basement like Lary probably does. I am, frankly, cursed.

"You got to control the hole," Lary tsks, pointing to his mouth.

"I have way more holes than you do," I remind him.

It's true, that's the curse. Extra holes. They can't all be empty at the same time, either. It's just not natural. It does not help, at all, to hear that my ex-boyfriend is dating a twenty-year-old contortionist (or whatever). For God's sake, when you break up with someone they should at least have the decency to die quietly while reaching for your photograph, especially after you declined Lary's heartfelt offer to have them assassinated. I swear to God, I don't know what's wrong with the world when a perfectly passable female like me ends up dateless for a six-month stretch. It's not like I don't get out there. It's not like I can't

Friends & Lovers

be easily found, clear as day, under my desk in the dark with brownie batter in my hair. Christ, what is wrong with people—are they blind? Come and get me.

Because odds are I can at least snag a bad one, and it used to be that even bad relationships were fun in their own way. I once dated a British bartender who lived in Grand Cayman. The odds of that lasting were about 80 points below leprechauns on the list of probabilities, but at least it got me out of the house. Way out. I can still remember the color of the ocean as the plane made its approach: pale blue like the knees of a child's dungarees. See what I mean; even when things don't stick, things stick.

"You gotta be like a screen door," Grant keeps telling me. "You gotta let things pass through you."

"Right," says Lary, who is such a cinder block nothing ever gets through him. You'd never find him with his head in his hands because the hole in his heart all of a sudden widened like the horizon one day. You'd never see him doing what he can to stuff it shut again. He and Grant both are tough as Teflon. Their hearts could deflect a shower of old power drills, I swear. They are such sea urchins—such crusty emotional acid vats—that I thank God for them every damn day.

"I love you guys," I mumble.

"Did you catch that?" Lary says.

"I didn't catch that," Grant says.

My words ricochet between them, not sticking. I smile, though, because even when things don't stick, things stick.

The Me in My Head

THE BRUISES ON MY ASS ARE NOT FROM HAVING hot buffalo sex with my ex-boyfriend Keiger, as Grant would have preferred to believe. Not that I have ever willingly shown Grant my ass—Lord, get that out of your head—but there's not much I can do when he keeps peeking through the curtains while I try on all the vintage cocktail dresses he picks out for me when we troll thrift stores.

"I hope you had some fun bruising up your ass like that," he'd said.

"Get out!" I shrieked at him, and he did, but not before handing me something his own mother had probably worn at a pool party when he was eight. Grant is always trying to dress me like his mother from the '70s, though, admittedly, she is a stylish woman.

"I have a picture of me and my mother both twirling batons, posing like this," Grant said, arching his back, kicking his leg up and extending his arm out front with his fingers flayed. "I will treasure it forever."

"Really?" I asked, almost actually kind of quasi-charmed at the thought of Grant as a young boy tossing batons with his mom. "When was the picture taken?"

"Last week," he answered, pitching me another cocktail dress.

I don't know who Grant sees when he looks at me, but these dresses would have fit me better back before I had bruises on my ass, back when I had an entirely different ass, one that weighed at least fifteen pounds less than the one I have now. That ass would look awesome in these cocktail dresses, which, of course, I bought on Grant's insistence. Now they're hanging in my closet with the rest of the stuff I won't wear but refuse to toss, clothes that still fit the me in my head, and as long as I don't try them on again, the me in my head will match the me in the mirror.

But it's just a matter of time before that illusion clashes with reality. Like the other day, when I went to Barnes & Noble with my girl. They have small chairs in the kids' section, sturdy little brightly colored Adirondack chairs with armrests and everything. When I looked at those chairs, it must not have occurred to me that I wasn't a child myself, because the me in my head had no problem with directing my butt to plunk itself right in one. The chair objected, though, and now I have these two bruises that run like stripes on either side of my rear, marking the spots where the sturdy little Adirondack armrests refused to allow my ass passage to the seat beneath them. The bruises are so straight they look like they've been drawn on by a plastic surgeon or something. "In order for the you in your head to match the you in reality," this plastic surgeon is saying, "you'll need to get rid of everything outside these lines."

Looking back, I suppose it was bound to happen. I mean, surely, eventually something was gonna occur to make me start seeing myself as I actually am, as opposed to the me I thought I was. Grant always says the truth will set people free, "but first it will piss them off." I wouldn't say I was pissed so much as just curious; like how long might I have gone, I thought, not knowing that I'm not the me I used to be, and who would it have harmed if I never came to know any differently?

Because what keeps coming up in my head, now that the me in

my head no longer occupies space there, is that photograph of Grant and his mother, the one where they're both posing with batons, their backs arched and their arms outstretched and their fingers gracefully flayed in front. Some people would look at that picture and probably see a seventy-eight-year-old grandmother and her mole-flecked, big-headed, twice-divorced, latent-gay son engaged in some tandem act of massive denial. I can hear the judgment right now. "Who do these two think they are? Do they not know how they look?"

But it's obvious these two don't care how they look to anybody but themselves and each other. In their minds they are still young and playful, and when I look at that picture, I see the majorette she used to be, and I see the incandescent child that Grant was as well. I see the elation on their faces, their love for each other, and the them that is in their heads. There is no reason why this perception can't absolutely be as valid as any other.

And when Grant kept handing me vintage little cocktail shifts that someone a lot cuter should wear, I had to admit I liked the me that was in Grant's head a lot better than the one I'm stuck with now. Seriously, when the you in your head disappears, it's highly recommended to have someone you love close by to replace it. Later, as we were driving around, he pointed out a George Bernard Shaw quote on a sign above a toy store. "We don't stop playing because we grow old," it read, "we grow old because we stopped playing."

"So snap out of it," Grant said. He was right. Just because your ass no longer fits in a child's chair doesn't mean the child in you is no longer there.

Friends & Lovers

Fresh vs. Frozen

IF GRANT'S GONNA DIE SOON LIKE HE SAYS HE IS, I hope he does it without making a mess. I seriously hate those messy-death deaths, though you can hardly avoid them anymore. It seems like every time you turn around, there's people falling from above and splattering at your feet. Or someone's getting beheaded in front of an audience of millions, and I can't think of a more embarrassing situation, really, than to have your head cut off in front of a camera, then to have that videotaped for any old ass to watch again and again. Jesus God.

But back to Grant. He went onto some Mexican Web site to take a twenty-page survey full of weird parapsychological questions, and at the end he was asked to click a button to discover the actual day of his death, which the Web site says will be next February, and Grant believes the Web site. I found this out when he hesitated to go skydiving with his friend Hector on Hector's twenty-fifth birthday last Sunday.

"Good for you," I told Grant, because at first I thought he was being sensible, which makes me wonder when the hell I'm ever gonna learn. I've known this man more than a decade now; this is a person who gave away all his possessions and moved to Mexico with nothing but a backpack full of prescription sunglasses, only to move back six months later because he got bored. Sense is the last thing to dictate Grant's decisions, followed only by the fear of death. Grant couldn't care less if he croaked this minute, I swear to God, which of course infuriates me, as I would miss the shit out of him if he died, and I think that merits some consideration in his decisions, such as the decision not to skydive. But no.

"Bitch, I've got four months left to live," he huffed, referring to the Web site results. "I ain't spending them in a wheelchair trying to operate the controls with my tongue. I got stuff to do."

"Well, goddamn, get the life insurance application then," I said. "If you're gonna croak in four months, you gotta make sure I'm cared for, not to mention your baby, which I plan to have so I can grow your replacement. So hurry up and knock me up. Gimme some sperm. I know you got it."

"Get it yourself," he said. "I donated twenty tubs of the stuff back in the '80s when I was working my way through seminary school."

It did not surprise me in the least that Grant financed Bible college by beating off to gay porn, but the new perspective on the cache of pre-  served sperm kind of threw me. I'd always known it was out there, but I never really thought of it as a resource until now. *Wow, perfectly good sperm,* I thought. People pay a lot of money for that.

"Really?" I said tentatively, because until then I didn't think I was serious; then my ovaries started speaking up, and I hadn't heard from them in years. "But that's expensive. Why should I pay for it when I know you're full of free sperm? You could do it right now. Go. Ask for a spare cup at the coffee counter."

Friends & Lovers

Grant shook his head. "You're gonna want the frozen stuff," he argued. "Of course I could give you sperm fresh from my body right now, but the frozen stuff is me from twenty years ago. I made a much better specimen then."

And here I had to agree with him, not that I have ever come into direct contact with any of Grant's sperm—though last year I did sit in the backseat of his Honda Element, which, wrung out, could probably produce enough to populate a planet—but I have been in contact with their result. His daughter, Mary Grace, is in her twenties and she qualifies as a walking goddess. And she's smart, too; she moved abroad when George W. got elected, for one. But she is a product of young sperm from a young Grant. I don't have the same selection. My selection is limited to old sperm from a young Grant or young sperm from an old Grant. Plus, I'm not at all convinced either wouldn't produce the fall of society, and I'm undecided over whether that would be a good or a bad thing.

Christ, I thought, clutching my head, *there are so many decisions that a responsible mother has to face these days.* Like, if I choose the old sperm from the young Grant, I can have it injected fairly innocuously, whereas if I choose the young sperm from the old Grant, I know he'll insist on implanting it using his own equipment. But then again, the frozen sperm isn't going anywhere, seeing as how it's frozen, whereas the fresh sperm, according to Grant, is due to go out of production next February.

"I pick the fresh sperm," I told Grant. "On one condition: You can't die. I'm not getting knocked up with your big-headed baby just so you can croak in three months. You at least have to be there when I pop. Beyond that, I'll assess your usefulness on a month-to-month basis. Deal?"

"Deal," he said.

Soon enough the day of Grant's preordained demise came, and all I have to say is if it were my last night to live, I wouldn't spend it behind the bar at The Local. But that's me.

"Come see me on my last night on Earth," he blared to anyone who would listen, because Grant is nothing if not above whoring his impending doom for a few extra nickels in the tip jar. I for one would have spent that time curled up under my sink or something, because I am nothing if not terrified of superstitions. In fact, I once saw a black cat cross my path, and three days later my own cat, Jethro, died.

Not that I blame the black cat. I blame myself for being afraid of the black cat, because the second I saw the black cat I started to fear what the hell was gonna happen, and while I was busy being afraid, I didn't notice my own cat missing until it was too late. So not only did I fear the black cat, I feared the fear, and a mind-set like that stirs up its own shit.

Anyway, Grant didn't die like he said he would. We were all waiting expectantly, but he didn't clutch his throat or get shot along with five others by an idiot in a black trench coat, or even trip and fall and impale his big head on a beer spigot. No. He just lived on like nothing important had happened at all, like there was no Mexican mystic who had ordained his death. The damn nerve of Grant, to live on without fear. Who spends his last night on Earth working like that?

Friends & Lovers

"Today I have been reborn," he said when he didn't die. "I am risen."

I guess that's what they say about near-death experiences; they change you. Grant says I've got nothing to fear, but he always says that. "Don't fear the truth," he always says, but it's not as easy as that, is it? Not only do people fear the truth, they fear the fear, and a mind-set like that stirs up its own shit.

"I think you should know I decided against having your baby," I informed him. "So I won't be growing your replacement after all."

"Your loss," he yawned.

The Replacements

WHEN I FIRST GAVE BIRTH, LARY PRACTICALLY BANNED me from the cement mausoleum he calls a home, so worried he was that I'd lactate all over his album covers or something. Not that I would ever, for a second, as an actual mother, think to bring a baby into Lary's Cave of Wet Concrete and Rusty Rails, but Lary was used to me as he knew me. He was not aware of the replacement that had taken my shape after I'd spawned. Case in point: It took him a while to notice there was now a definite absence of alcohol in our interactions. Don't get me wrong, alcohol is very important. If not for alcohol, I wouldn't have had half the sex I did in my twenties, and I certainly would not have gotten knocked up. But once you become a mother, booze loses its usefulness because you don't want to be the mom on *Cops* who greets the squad car in a bathrobe and a beer in her hand, slurring, "Thass my baby bleedin' at the bottom of the stairs." So you replace booze with something else, like coffee.

That's what parents do, they make replacements. I remember my mother's old diabetic neighbor, Tilly, who lived in the trailer next door and hung out on her patio all day to drink bourbon and air out the stitches on her leg stumps. One time she caught me as I took out the trash and invited me over to view her collection of crafts in her trailer, the atmosphere of which was so heavy with booze breath it smelled like an operating mustard-gas factory.

Her walls were lined with bookcases packed with nothing but homemade toilet paper cozies. The cozies were the half-Barbie-doll and half-yarn-knit-hoop-skirt kind, the idea being that the skirt would fit around an extra roll of toilet paper so it could be decoratively displayed in your bathroom. Tilly was pretty proud of her work. A tub of bisected Barbie doll parts spilled out from under her dining table, which itself was dotted with bourbon bottles. She wheeled over and fumbled with one.

"Drink?" she offered, knocking the bottle over with her hand.

"Let me," I said, rising from my seat to help her.

The desire to escape was powerful—for one, it was obvious her cats had mistaken the tub of Barbie parts for their litter box. But Tilly needed company, and I was as good a replacement as any for the grown daughter who'd dropped Tilly off after her surgery and hadn't been seen since. Her name was Theresa, Tilly told me, and she was studying at the same college I attended. The sorrow in Tilly's voice when she spoke of her daughter was so evident that I let Tilly dote on me until it was time to wheel her drunk ass back out to the patio. "Take these," she said as I left, handing me an armful of cozies. "You can never have enough."

Yes, you can never have enough toilet paper cozies, especially if toilet paper cozies are all you have. Tilly's daughter, Theresa, by the way, became a successful art broker and is a mother herself now. These days I often think about Theresa and how she fares when she thinks of her mom. Because before I became a mother myself, it was no problem to remember Tilly as she was when I left her: alone, legless, and ignored by a daughter. Now, though . . . now that memory is simply unbearable, and it has to be replaced.

The Mattress

SINCE WHEN DO MATTRESSES MATTER SO MUCH? Because all of a sudden, it seems like every single person I know has become a complete mattress pussy. The other day, I went to The Local to yell at Keiger some more, and somehow instead ended up asking him in a quasi-civil manner how he's been lately. He launched into this starry-eyed soliloquy about his brand-new king-size mattress and all the zillion-thread-count bedsheets he'd imported from a company in Egypt that excavates them out from under dead pharaohs or something. And I don't know about you, but the last thing a girl wants to hear is how happy her ex-boyfriend is sleeping all alone (hopefully) in his big, new, pussy-plush fucking super spring that he probably paid more for than he did on all their past dates combined. So, of course, I had to start yelling at him again.

"You could call me, you know," I heard him say as I stormed out.

Not really. I erased his number off my phone and threw his house key in the river.

So I called Lary instead. "What the hell is it about mattresses?" I asked him. Lary's a good person to ask. His place is little more than a mosquito-infested concrete bunker (although he did add air-conditioning recently), with corroded floors that have stuff growing through the cracks, yet right in the middle of everything, almost like a throne, is this king-size bed with a cushy-ass mattress so thick and pillowy it could probably absorb a fleet of crashing aircraft. He does not even have curtains—or windows, for that matter, depending on the destructiveness of his mood—yet he invested more money purchasing that mattress than he did when he bought the entire dilapidated spider hole he calls a home.

"It's great," Lary swears. "Since I've been sleeping on that mattress, I have fewer dreams about carnage, rape, and mutilation." Right. As if he'd ever consider fewer thoughts of rape and mutilation a positive by-product.

When I was a kid, mattresses were like the last thing my family thought about. Probably because mattresses are the hardest things to move in and out of a house, and since we were always moving in and out of houses, we usually just left ours behind. My mother was always into beds that served other purposes, too, like her "trundle bed" phase. A trundle bed is actually two twin beds, one on top of the other, with the upper one acting as a sofa of sorts, while the lower one awaits underneath it on wheels, so it can pop up and surprise visitors with a rest area that is as comfortable as a pit full of chips collected from the Petrified Forest.

The only problem is that we never had guests. So these wondrous conversions inevitably became our actual bedroom furniture, at first just until we could replace our real mattress, but since we always moved again before that could happen, we eventually dropped the pretense. My room had the "corner unit" as my mother liked to call it, an L-shaped thing that was joined at the bend by an end table that also served as an alcove to stash the front half of each cot. It did not have fitted sheets, but rather upholstered pad covers made from that bristly, orange synthetic '70s material spun from volcanic magma or whatever.

Sleeping on that overnight thoroughly stippled my skin, so that for the first two periods of class I always looked like I was fighting a flea-allergy outbreak. Complain as I might, though, my sister Kim had it worse. She got the sofa bed. The mattress on that was half as thick as the kind they provide criminals in the county jail. Worse, it was a "love seat" sofa bed, which means it pulled out to provide less width than the backseat of our Fairlane.

But hey, when it closed up, it automatically converted her room to an additional den, or "salon," a term preferred by my mother, who envisioned dinner parties after which women would retire to the salon to compare curtain patterns so the men could sit in the living room and belch among themselves. I think my mother was always entertaining thoughts of entertaining people, that one day we might live in one place long enough to have, like, guests. Our home seemed to be in constant preparation for that, all our rooms ready to convert into a network of seating areas to welcome company that never came. Looking back, I wish for her sake that we'd had some.

So I was in that mind-set as I drove around aimlessly, fuming about Keiger, only it wasn't so aimless because all of a sudden I was pulling into his driveway. I just miss him so much, I miss how his arms enclose me and fold me all up in him, converting me into something that can stand another day like the one I just had. I miss his hands on my face, and the way he murmured in my ear. "Don't you worry," he'd say, "you're strong." Ha! So strong that here I am, staring at his door. Who's the mattress now? But still I stood there, because he was inside, all alone in that stupid big-ass bed, and I just don't want the people I love to hope for company that never comes anymore.

Friends & Lovers

On the House

I NEVER KNOCKED ON KEIGER'S DOOR. I turned around, went back to my car, and went to The Local instead. Just because Keiger and I don't date anymore doesn't mean I can't continue to go to The Local and act like I own the place. I was there the other day, telling everyone everything was on the house. I really enjoy doing that. People are so grateful to me, and then put off by Keiger when he swoops in afterward to make them pay anyway. I always leave feeling like I've done a service to society.

"Everything's on the house," I was hollering, but the only person to hear me was Grant, who works there. The bar was empty, but it was early yet. I'd called beforehand to warn Keiger I was coming in. "I'll be there in a few minutes, so if you're gonna leave, do it now, because I don't want you humiliating me by running out the back door the second I show up." Not that getting dumped isn't humiliating enough.

Surprisingly, though, Keiger did not leave when I got there. Instead he stayed put and complained about how, seven months ago when we broke up after he failed to call me for five weeks straight, it wasn't all his fault. "You could have called me, you know," he said. "What kind of relationship is it if I have to call you all the time?"

"Keiger, just for the record," I sighed, "you don't have to call me all the time. But you do have to call me more than *never again*."

Anyway, the real reason I was supposedly there was to talk to Grant about Lary, whom we hadn't seen in some time. Earlier, over breakfast at the Majestic, we'd concluded that Lary's behavior super definitely matched all the warning signs of meth addiction this time, as we figure we're still very attuned to these signs ever since we staged that intervention for our other friend. We hear she's doing really well, and she might even get her job back. This outcome of course makes us think we're experts on what's best for people.

Now it seems Lary has totally withdrawn from us, which is a symptom. Sure, he says he's working all the time, but addicts lie. And the last time I saw him, he looked like he'd been scraped off the bottom of a boat. Of course, that's par for Lary, but his teeth, I'm telling you, had the makings of total meth mouth if you ask me. He claimed it was just griddlies from the overtoasted bagel he recently ate, but I'm not so sure.

"Obviously, it's time that we break into his house again," I told Grant. He agreed, of course. If there's one thing I respect about Grant, it's his concern for his fellow friends.

Second-Floor Conversion

THE FIRST THING I NOTICED ABOUT LARY'S PLACE was that his trailer was not yet on top of the warehouse where he lives. One day years ago, after he had combined the effects of alcohol and crane operating, he'd awakened to find a truck on his roof. After that he decided he liked things on his roof, and started putting all kinds of crap up there, including, but not limited to, an entire life-size plastic lawn nativity scene, various tires, birdcages, a herd of feral cats, and, on and off, that same truck.

Next he concluded that he'd like to put an actual trailer up there as well, because it would make a nice second-floor conversion. He says all he has to do is drill a big hole in his ceiling as well as through the underside of the trailer, then bolt one of those wrought-iron spiral staircases into place, and *voila,* an economic upper wing. I have to tell you, if he pulls that off I will be so jealous my head will hemorrhage.

"Please put it on my roof instead," I begged him. My house is much more suited to sit under a trailer, if you ask me. First of all, it's hardly bigger than one, so it would serve as the proper understated pedestal and not detract from the magnificence of the Airstream. Lary's dilapidated old warehouse, on the other hand, is so huge and its roof so high that an Airstream on top of it would just sit there like a silver boil and probably hardly be noticeable, especially considering all the other stuff that's up there.

"The roof is where I put all the stuff I really value," he says.

Remember that Lary is an event rigger by profession, and not just any rigger; he's like the master Jedi rigger that other riggers bow before. Whatever you need done, Lary can figure out a way to do it, including, but not limited to, probably time travel. This is why huge companies pay him tons of money to accomplish the impossible at their conventions. For example, if plans call for a Ferris wheel suspended over a lake in the center of a previously lakeless sports arena, Lary is the one they finally approach to get it done once everyone else says it can't be done.

"Get the hell out of there," Lary bitched to us over the phone, because of course we couldn't break into his house without calling him to report on our progress. He was in Hawaii, or said he was, working a job. "What's this crap in your freezer?" I asked. "I don't know—food?" he replied. Like hell it is, I thought. For one, it was green and pasty. "Is this food?" I called to Grant, but he was busy in Lary's bathroom stealing all his cotton swabs. I checked the pressure cooker, and there was nothing inside but the entire supply of Latin Xanax he got from me for helping me haul my trailer out of the irrigation ditch that one time. Finally we had decided to leave, concluding that Lary's real drugs were too well hidden for us to find—besides, I don't even know what crystal meth looks like (is it green and pasty?)—when suddenly I caught sight of some thongs hanging on the branches of a plant by the bed.

"What the hell are these thongs in the plants?" I asked Lary.

"They're mine," he insisted.

"Like hell they are," I said. They looked like they were made to fit a hipless Romanian gymnast, not Lary, who has the passable ass of an old rock guitarist. Then Grant and I investigated further and found all kinds of curious feminine amenities tucked away in drawers and medicine cabinets and such. *Oh my God!* I realized. It turns out Lary isn't addicted to drugs. It turns out he's kind of in a quasi-relationship.

I couldn't believe it. Who knew Lary was capable? I would have punched him affectionately right then, but he was in Hawaii staying at the Four Seasons, probably with his new girlfriend. Evidently word of his patented brand of rigger madness had reached the people with real money, and he'd been hired to simulate a giant-scale, authentic volcanic eruption or something for some huge convention out there. Of course the idea of making his own magma was irresistible to Lary. "It's incredible, like the earth is violently puking," he says. "I can't wait to see it happen with a real volcano." He says that last part like he'll have some say in it, which, knowing Lary, he probably will.

I should have known better than to doubt him. I remember I scoffed at him when he said he was going to steal a billboard from the freeway once, and the next time I went to his place to water his plants, there it was: a massive highway sign that read JESUS WAS A VEGETAR-IAN taking up most of his warehouse. The billboard pissed him off, he said, and it had to come down. He must have climbed an edifice twenty flights high to pull that off.

So if Lary says he's going to put a trailer on his house, he probably will. I'm especially looking forward to the part about the wrought-iron spiral staircase. I know those things are easy to put up and take down because my mother once stole one from one of our many rented residences. They're not much more than twisted ladders, really, and all it took was a good shaking and it practically popped right off the brackets into her hands. It probably helped that my sisters and I used to hang and climb on it like on an upended monkey bar, loosening it to a good degree. That was a big heist for her. The last I saw of that staircase was decades ago in the shed she kept in back of the trailer she'd bought just north of the Tijuana border. That shed is where she kept all the stuff she really valued.

It turned out she never needed any of it. If she had known Lary, though, he could have put all the pieces together to make her a home of her own. He can rig anything. He can make the impossible possible. He can put a trailer on his house and then turn around and ask me if I'd like one on mine.

It occurred to me right then that it's probably possible for people to go through life and never have a home, even though they may spend every second surrounded by walls. In the end it's not until they start collecting things they really value, and keeping them someplace safe, that their home starts to take shape. And now Lary is sharing his home with his new love. He'll deny it, but all addicts lie.

Friends & Lovers

All Your Lovely Crap

GRANT AND DANIEL AND I TRY TO PROVOKE Lary with torments that he might be dating his own daughter, seeing as how he's prone to all those prolonged fits of forgetfulness. He accomplishes the most complicated feats during these fogs, too, like erecting that entire network of scaffolding in his kitchen. He had no idea how it came to be. He just claims to have awakened to find it like that, as if arranged there by a playful poltergeist. So fathering a child would have been effortless in comparison, because the early '80s, what with the easy proliferation of LSD and other hallucinogens, was probably just one big long stupor for Lary.

But it's been a while since Lary woke up to find himself underneath teetering industrial trace material. These days it's all been replaced by those thongs and other curious feminine amenities, such as the set of amputated cat testicles she keeps with her in a jar of formaldehyde (when we heard about that, we were doubly certain those two were related), but no matter the nature of the stuff strewn about his place, Lary's response to it is still the same. "Where did this crap come from?" he complains. "None of it's mine."

"What're you bitchin' about?" Grant asks him. For one, Grant points out, Lary's got a hot young girlfriend these days, and some pay a huge cost to have one of those, whereas the cost to Lary has been relatively little. It's not like she demands constant body rubs and gourmet meals coupled with a new car every month. Amazingly, all she seems to require is a place to put her underwear. You know, other than the plants. Occasionally she'll ask Lary to marry her, but he suffers no real punishment when he counters that with an offer to adopt her instead, and she actually laughed when he responded to her request for a baby with, "Sure, it would make a great parting gift." All that plus she's covered in tattoos and keeps her cat's neutered nuts in a jar!

"Christ, Lary," says Grant, "she's the ideal woman."

It's the crap, though, that is always the cost. If you ask me, I'm amazed people think they can get through a relationship without encountering any of the other person's crap at some level. And I'm not just talking about tangible stuff, like Kotex and cat balls, but every single cruddy nugget of emotional torture you had to encounter in your life in order to claw yourself to the relatively safe level of livability you've managed to reach so far. The crap is there, admit it, and trying to keep it hidden just makes it all the more ugly once it inevitably rears itself.

Take that time in college when I dated that Bible-thumping rich boy, who dumped me like a load of toxic waste—took back his Bible and everything—leaving my barely saved soul sitting there on the cusp of relapse back into Satan's cesspool. Until then I was thinking, Great! This guy's a Jesus freak, so by nature he's supposed to be forgiving and not all that bothered by the fact that, until I met him, I'd been pursuing the reputation of a four-star slut. I thought I could wrap all my lovely crap up in a box, slap a bow on it, and hand it to him like a damn door prize. I was even kind of proud of the fact that it was bound to be such a big box, too, for such a young person.

Friends & Lovers

But it turns out the last thing he wanted was to become co-owner of all my crap, emotional or otherwise. I could have kept it all hidden, but if I did I'd probably be living in Colorado right now, the wife of an overly religious car salesman. So you see, keeping it hidden just makes it all the more ugly. That's why it's best to just get it out there, all your lovely crap. Fling it about like confetti. Hang it from the branches of potted plants if you have to.

Full of It

///

For the first time in my life, I can say Grant is literally full of crap and Lary literally is not. But before I go any further, I'd just like to note that I am as confused as anyone as to why my friends feel the need to update me on their regularity, Daniel included. He just called me all googly about the lovely light-headedness he felt all day after giving himself a coffee enema.

"Promise me you'll try this," he insisted. I promised him that the very last thing I'll ever do with a pot of decent Costa Rican is shoot it up my ass, but Daniel was too busy chasing butterflies by then, or whatever other beautiful pursuits the clarity of consciousness is supposed to reveal to you as part of the benefits of flooding your butt with caffeine.

This has been going on since I met them. It's one of the things they all have in common, this fascination with flushing their systems. "John Wayne died with forty pounds of crap in his colon," Daniel says. "Did you know that's true?" I do not know if that's true, but I do know that Daniel has told me this tidbit roughly twenty-six times over the course of our friendship as though it were the first time I've ever heard it, and about a million other times as part of what he considers a normal conversation.

"John Wayne was literally full of shit," Daniel says.

Grant is no better. Soon after I met him nine years ago, he became kind of addicted to colonics. I don't remember if he was gay by then or not, but if he wasn't, I guess this habit might have served as a sort

Friends & Lovers

223

of surrogate for his future leanings. Anyway, it all sounded suspicious to me, as the place he went to have them administered wasn't even a clinic. "Don't you need like a license or something to shove tubes up people's asses?" I asked, but Grant did not know and did not care. He was too busy feeling the effects of having been flushed. Colonics, in case you don't know, cost more than a full body massage. In Grant's case, as with any addiction, it got a little ugly. Pretty soon he was getting them done by some guy in a van, practically. He might as well have been hosing himself out at the do-it-yourself car wash on DeKalb Avenue.

Believe it or not, Lary is into that stuff, too. Barring all the bourbon, acid, mail-order amphetamines, and painkillers pirated from a willing cancer-stricken friend, Lary can be downright health conscious when it comes to putting things in his body. Whenever I go to his place to mooch food under the guise of tending to his (still missing) cat, the closest I can find to junk food is a bag of pistachios. So when he announced he was about to, at the insistence of his new girlfriend, undergo his first colonic, I was a little surprised he'd never had one, as there are few firsts left for Lary.

"You won't believe the stuff that comes out of you!" Grant squealed. "You're literally gonna see crayons you ate as a kid."

"Oh, my God," I said, "you see it?"

"All that stuff that's been stuck in you your whole life, you literally see it flow by in the tube."

Lary was excited, wondering if there'd be toy soldiers, heirloom jewelry, or perhaps even his missing cat. "Think of the mysteries that can be solved," he chimed, as though Jimmy Hoffa were up in there somewhere.

Weeks earlier, there'd been another somewhat mystery, when Grant had awakened a few days after a minor car accident to find that he couldn't move or breathe, not literally, but close enough. So, of course, the first thing Grant did was call Lary, and, of course, the first thing Lary did was drive right over, pick Grant up, and take him to a yard sale.

"Did you check out the clothes rack?" Grant mewled from the periphery, as Lary had propped him against the tire well of his truck to ensure he got a good view. To Lary's credit, though, Grant had insisted he was fine as long as he remained motionless while leaning just so. "That way I can almost breathe. I'll be fine."

"He's not fine!" shrieked Mary Jane, a nurse who is also Lary's perfectly lovely ex-girlfriend. They had called her when it seemed that paralysis had started to set in. "He could have a lacerated liver or a collapsed lung! You need to get him to the emergency room right away!"

It turns out that the car accident had broken a few of Grant's ribs, which resulted in so much swelling that it caused an obstruction in his intestines. In short, Grant was suffering from a bionic case of killer constipation, literally. Under Lary's coaching ("Cry like a baby!"), Grant was able to procure some respectably potent painkillers. "I love yer ass," he's been saying to me lately, all painless and happy to be past the crap in his life, literally and otherwise. He thwacks me on the rear, "I literally love yer ass."

Friends & Lovers

Soft Ornaments

I DON'T KNOW WHAT IT SAYS ABOUT A CHRISTMAS tree if a damn cat can knock it down, but surely that can't be a good sign. Maybe I shouldn't have my tree on top of a table, but my window is five feet off the floor and it's the only way I can think of to make the tree look proportional from the street. So I put it on the table and figured, since it's fake and full of electrical wires, maybe my cats would leave it alone. But my new cat, Petal, must be half raccoon; she even looks a little raccoon-ish, and I, well, I wouldn't have picked her out if I'd had a choice. Petal picked me; she kept showing up at my door to remind me I was hers, that she'd picked me and there was not a lot I could do about it because I was hers and that's just the way it is. So here I have this half-raccoon cat who will climb anything, which is why I keep finding the tree on my bed when I get home.

Not that she drags it there. My bed is next to the table where I keep the tree, so all Petal has to do is knock the tree over and my bed catches it. My Christmas tree has bounced on my bed more than I have, which is saying something, so for this reason Milly is only allowed to put "soft ornaments" on it. Even I didn't know what the hell I meant by that, but remarkably Milly had no problem figuring out that plenty of soft things serve quite nicely as ornaments—finger puppets, pot holders, cookies, and old prescription-medicine canisters to name a few. I must admit it all looks kind of pretty. To be truthful, though, Milly could hang ornaments she made out of her own earwax and I'd still gurgle with pride like the pathetic hen that I am. "See the angel Milly made for the tree?" I boasted to Grant and Keiger. "Is that not amazing?"

"It's a wad of dental floss," Grant observed. He was not amazed at all.

"It's not even knotted," Keiger added, though he was a tiny tad amazed.

"This is art!" I told them. "I swear to Jesus God, the wonder of authentic, God-given genius is totally wasted on you bunch of booger-eating plebians. Why do I even bother?" I would have continued, throwing in how Grant's idea of passable party fare is pig's feet and Cheetos, while Keiger's own Christmas tree is little more than an ailing spider plant festooned with two anemic strands of tinsel, but just then my tree got knocked down again and I had to rush to make sure my new cat wasn't trapped or, worse, electrocuted.

"You need to kill that cat," Grant said, but I know he only says stuff like this to dissuade me from ever asking him to pet-sit for me again. He still claims to be traumatized from the last time eight years ago, when he cat-sat for me and the late Lucy, my treasured toothless old alley-cat rescue, tried to sleep on his head. Normally I would have said it served him right for having such a huge head, but Lucy slept on my own head every night and it didn't occur to me until then that anyone would mind having a soft, furry purring thing keeping their head warm all night. I tell you, it was downright nice having Lucy on my head unless I had to move or something, in which case she'd dig her claws into my skull, but other than that all I had to do was stay perfectly still and she'd lie there on my forehead as peacefully as a

Friends & Lovers

toothless, tuna-smelling toupee, hardly interrupting my oxygen supply at all.

"I mean it," Grant insisted, "kill that cat."

"I can't kill Petal," I said. It's true. Petal picked me as her owner, plain and simple.

Keiger was silent. Concerning my two cats, Keiger is unashamedly biased with his affections, bestowing most of them on Tinkerbell, my sixteen-year-old midget Persian who, until recently, had a skin condition that made her hair fall out in clumps. But since meeting Keiger, her hair puffed all up again, so Keiger nicknamed her "P. Diddy." I have never seen a cat so in love as Tinkerbell is with Keiger. She quakes with joy every time he comes over, wraps herself around his neck, nibbles his ears and kisses his eyelids. It's a wonder to behold. After Keiger and I broke up, Tinkerbell practically lay around bawling with her paws outstretched. Not even Petal could pull her out of her malaise. Finally there was nothing for me to do but to drive back to Keiger's and show up on his doorstep again, this time to remind him that he was mine, that I'd picked him, and he was mine and there was not a lot he could do about it. I love him and that's just the way it is. He didn't seem all that convinced at first, so I wrapped myself around his neck, all soft and purring, and he wisely stayed perfectly still, knowing, I'm sure, that if he tried to move I'd have dug my claws into his skull.

Power Couple

IT'S KIND OF HARD TO CONVINCE PEOPLE you're part of a power couple when your boyfriend is elbow deep into a toilet every morning. "You own this place," I tell Keiger. "Isn't there someone you can pay to clean the toilets?"

Keiger snaps off his rubber gloves. "I'm part-owner," he corrects me.

"Ain't no other owner here cleaning the toilets," I say.

We're at The Local the morning after what appears to have been an incredibly busy night, and the place smells like an ashtray eaten by somebody with bionic halitosis. Debris is everywhere, including the butts of about eight million cigarettes, a truckload of french fries bonded to the floor under a crust of dried beer, and, oddly, one brightly colored Christmas tree skirt. No underwear, though. Not this time. By five o'clock, this entire place will be remarkably clean—not eat-off-the-floor clean, but clean-enough-to-want-to-come-back clean—a transformation that always amazes me. No matter how trashed The Local gets the night before—and believe me, I've seen it so bad they should have marked off the area with crime-scene tape—it's always ready for business the next day.

Keiger himself cleans the toilets every morning because, he says, it's the worst job in the place and he would not ask it of his employees. As his girlfriend, currently, I consider it my duty to serve as a distraction by demanding he blow off work and come get coffee with me and Grant, but he rarely falls for it. I, though, have fallen for him. I must say I do like a laboring man. A suit-and-tie guy with a cell phone fused to his fist does nothing for me except exacerbate my TMJ with yawns. But put that same guy in leather gloves and goggles and have him sand down a door or something, and I'll be stuck to him like putty. Still, though, there are certain standards to consider. We are now, after all, a power couple.

"This is not how a power couple behaves," I complained to Lary later. Lary had no idea what a power couple was, and neither did I until someone told me that we could probably expect access to all the roped-off areas at society events and such, since Keiger is a successful business owner and I was voted "best columnist" in the city. This came about because the small paper I wrote for was bought by a much bigger paper, which means I'm now a columnist for a major-city newspaper, and even though I don't yet have the major-city salary to match, I figure I have certain responsibilities. For example, if Keiger ever succumbs to my begging and hires me to bartend, then I plan to wash my work apron at least once a month, as opposed to my former regimen with the airlines, which was never. Keiger suggests I also put some effort into actually working, as opposed to all the effort I put into avoiding it, but I don't want to go changing now that I'm all successful and shit.

"Power couple, my ass," Lary griped. "I will make certain that doesn't happen." He blathered about how he was gonna have to stage another drastic interruptive measure like he and Grant did two years ago when they held the "Hollis Gillespie Heifer Intervention Convention" after I gained thirty pounds. Daniel mixed the mimosas, and all of them instructed our friends to bring Krispy Kremes, fried chicken, chocolate-covered butter sticks, and any other fat-laden chow they could think of to help me celebrate my last communal wallow in slop before my mandatory starvation period set in. Everybody also came equipped with diet books. Lary brought a pair of pliers ("in case I need to wire your damn jaw shut") and a Web site address from which I could supposedly buy Internet amphetamines. Attendees placed bets on how long it would take me to lose the weight. It took me sixteen months.

"Whew," Grant said. "I was starting to worry you turned into a cow and were gonna stay that way."

Grant is starting his new diet, which consists solely of cayenne pepper, lemon juice, and mid-grade maple syrup. It's supposed to make him euphoric by the third day and hallucinate by the seventh, not to mention twenty pounds lighter. As the subject of a lot of my columns, he wants to ensure he strikes a respectable presence. "I'm having crazy dreams," he reported of the diet's effects. "Last night I dreamt neon blue rats were attacking our arms. Then my teeth fell out like piano keys, and then The Local fell a-fucking-part. The whole place just disintegrated and we couldn't do anything to keep it together."

"I'm not too worried about The Local," I said, and I didn't have to tell him why. It's because Keiger is running The Local, and he is really good at keeping things from falling apart, me included. In fact, being held together by Keiger is one of my favorite ways to spend the day.

"C'mon!" I keep coaxing Keiger. "It's a great afternoon! Let's get out. We should make an appearance. We're a power couple now."

Friends & Lovers

"Power couple, my ass," he says, handing me a toilet brush, which, as always, I ignore. Like I said, I can't go changing now that I'm all successful and shit.

UPWARD MOBILITY

It's funny the things that end your life. For me it happened when I accidentally almost ran down a crack addict in my neighborhood. "Bleachy-haired honky bitch!" he yelled at me as he shuffled out of my way. That encounter inspired a passage in my newspaper column, which in turn inspired a book about me and my friends, and now my life is over—or at least my life as it was is over. This is even more eventful than the time Lary was selling autographed pictures of Jesus on eBay, because now he's autographing pictures of himself, and it's almost like he doesn't know the difference.

"You've created a monster," says Grant, calling me from The Local where Lary was holding an impromptu signing of the book that features

him like the rock star he always thought he was. He captions his signature with, "The clown carries a gun."

For the past few years, my column had been running every week in Creative Loafing, *Atlanta's major weekly. Every week I pressed Send and forgot about it. Somewhere in the back of my head I knew it was out there published for everyone to read, but my standard of living stayed the same. I paddled along at the same panic level as ever, it just didn't dawn on me that an under-swell was brewing. Amazingly, my editor Suzanne published the stuff I wrote, even that legendary "Lary likes to masturbate by slamming his dick with the Bible" column.*

And then Bleachy-Haired Honky Bitch *came out, and an* Entertainment Weekly *writer showered it with accolades while pointing out, among other things, that I'd made my living as a flight attendant even though I was terrified to fly. After that my cover was completely blown. There was no going back.*

The Good Brother

THANK GOD GRANT'S BROTHER MIKE DIDN'T DIE, that's all I have to say. Grant himself didn't seem all that alarmed by the message from his mother, which he received once we landed in Los Angeles, and which, Grant said, basically imparted the news that Mike had died, but the message alarmed the holy hell out of me.

I should have remembered it was relayed to me through Grant, who himself is given to exaggeration, which, on top of his own mother's flair for the dramatic, meant Mike was probably home nursing a hangnail, but still. Mike is our business manager—mine and Grant's—having guided us through the tricky waters of Hollywood to our film deal, which is no small feat considering Grant and I are each as Hollywood-savvy as baboons. Plus, I am secretly in love with Mike, Mike being the non-gay quasi-equivalent to Grant, minus the huge freckly head and bad eyesight, so you can't be joking around with me about that.

"Christ," I shrieked, "what the hell do you mean Mike died? You can't say that! What happened?"

I refused to unlock Grant's side of the rental car until he gave me an explanation, but that was no threat since we'd gotten another PT Cruiser, and this one, I swear to God, was the bright yellow of a bad urine specimen. Grant had already refused to set foot in it. It was bad enough, he said, that he had to drive to the airport in Atlanta with me that morning in my own Cruiser, which he ridicules, but now he is expected to drive through West Hollywood with me in this piss-colored car? "I don't think so," he said, shaking his head with the phone still against his ear.

This is when I knew Mike didn't really die, because if his brother was really dead, even *Grant* would not have had the emotional stoniness to complain about the kind of car we got. So hallelujah. Mike is the only brother out of all my friends' brothers who provides me a decent foil for my secret affections. For example, Daniel's brother is more gay than Daniel is himself, if that's even possible, and Lary won't introduce me to his.

Still, though, we didn't really know what had happened to Mike, other than a message from Grant's mother, who said he'd been rushed to the hospital. After Grant finally deigned to seat himself in the piss-colored car, he started demon-dialing to discover what happened. Between leaving messages, Grant surmised that if Mike didn't make it, he could move to Colorado and commence helping his sister-in-law raise his nephew.

At this I thought, Lord Jesus God, let that man live. Not because Grant wouldn't make a decent father—on the contrary, his penchant for Mexican busboys aside, Grant is a great father, as evidenced by the perfectly normal and industrious daughter he sired and helped raise back in the day before he started having sex with men—but because if Grant moved to Colorado, I would have a harder time haranguing him than usual. My ability to harangue Grant is basically what gets me out of bed each morning.

But Grant, ever selfish, wasn't thinking of me. When he finally reached his brother, he'd already figured out how he was going to step in and take over Mike's role in his Colorado household.

Mike, it turned out, had had pneumonia, which was exacerbated, I'm sure, by his inability to stop working. Even as Grant called to inquire as to his condition, Mike had his own inquiries about our trip to Los Angeles, because the fact is we would not even have been there if not for Mike. It was Mike, who owns his own media company, who brokered film rights for me. It turns out a film project is a tricky process, and a half-dozen times, at least, I would have let it die on the vine like I hear so many of these things do. But Mike is the one who kept it alive. He navigated all the industry ministrations to the point where here we were again, in Hollywood, about to take another meeting at the Warner Bros. Studio.

Mike, sick as he was, talking to us from his hospital bed (probably), was characteristically more excited about our upcoming meeting than he was concerned about his own condition. "It's alive," he kept saying of our deal, sounding a little like Dr. Frankenstein. "It's alive!"

"Ask him how the hell he is," I shouted at Grant.

"He ain't gonna die," Grant hollered back at me.

He damn well better not die, I thought.

Upward Mobility

L.A. Lary

HERE IS WHAT I KNOW ABOUT LOS ANGELES so far: Lary could live here. I know this because he kept repeating it. "I could live here," he said after his third cappuccino at the Grove, a famous outdoor market that happens to be around the corner from our motel. In Atlanta I had never once seen Lary drink a cappuccino—he usually likes his coffee black as a bowling ball and just as thick—but since coming here he's been sucking down cappuccinos like liquid oxygen. "I could definitely live here," he said again.

"Who *are* you?" I asked, because I've known Lary for fourteen years and, believe me, I've seen some personalities emerge from him—like Evil Otis, the personality that occasionally lands him in jail for throwing things at police cars and copulating in public—but this Lary, this *L.A. Lary*, is unknown to me.

"Have I met you?" I asked, but he was busy. Some professional L.A. photographer had plucked him from the crowd and was in the process of discovering him. Lary gamely smiled his wicked, piranha-fish smile as the camera snapped away. I had never seen Lary act natural in front of a camera before. In his driver's license photo, for example, he looks like a stroke victim. On purpose.

"Do we know him?" I asked Daniel and Grant. But Daniel had his head buried inside a watermelon, the only thing he'd eaten since the plane landed two days prior. And Grant was busy sending the sonic gay vibe to every Mexican busboy in southern California.

I thought Lary would have taken to L.A. like a baby to barbed wire. Of the four of us—me, Daniel, Grant, and Lary—I am the only one who kind of quasi used to live here. I was born just up the way in Burbank, but I hadn't been back until Jay Leno had me on his show. It turns out the hospital where I was born is right across the street from the NBC studios. No one seemed as marveled by that as me.

I know everyone needs to have been born somewhere, and maybe it's normally not that big a deal for them to see where it happened on occasion, but it seriously did not occur to me until the limo was pulling into the guard post at NBC that, hey, looky there, that hospital across the street is the same one listed on my birth certificate. Flukes, really, being there then and having been before. In the latter case my parents had been driving home after visiting a relative nearby, when all of a sudden my mother doubled over, figuring she'd eaten some bad fish, but it turns out it was just me wanting to be born early. "It was like you jumped out of me all on your own," she used to tell me, "like you sure were in a hurry to get somewhere."

She was from Kansas and my dad was from Alabama, and they'd met at a cocktail party six months after she'd graduated from UCLA and were married six months after that. She didn't know he'd been fired from his third job selling trailers until they'd returned from their Las Vegas honeymoon, but by that time she was already pregnant with my brother. I guess it says something about my mother that, in the late '50s and knocked up at that, she could land a corporate job as a mathematician at IBM. "People do what they need to do," she used to say. I didn't yet know that it is, in fact, rare to find a person with that quality, a person who does what needs to be done.

Upward Mobility

That's why I asked Lary to go to L.A. with me. If nothing else, he gets things done, as almost all of his personalities are immensely productive. He shows up at The Local with curls of wood shavings clinging to his clothes and dried plaster in his hair, all remnants of having done something, though what it was is often, even to him, a mystery. "What'd you do today?" I asked him once as I brushed shrapnel off his clothing. "I don't know," he answered, "but my neighbor's chimney is missing." I figured he would come in handy in case the movie studio executives changed their minds and canceled our meeting later that afternoon, leaving us no choice but to break into their headquarters and threaten detonation until they agreed to our terms. But that was the Atlanta Lary. This other Lary, this L.A. Lary, I wasn't expecting.

After the photographer finished, we hopped in the car so Lary could drive us to some thrift stores, because L.A. Lary likes to drive. But soon we hit La Brea, where traffic was stuck in Formica it was so slow, and there we stayed, suspended, like the Precambrian relics touted in the billboard advertising the Le Brea Tar Pits. "Look, Lary," we joked, pointing at the tar pits, "isn't that where you were born?"

But as we laughed I looked over and saw immediately that L.A. Lary was gone. Atlanta Lary was back. "This blows," Lary groused at the insufferable traffic. "I could never live here."

Blind

///

WE'VE BEEN IN L.A. ONLY FOUR DAYS and already Daniel has whored himself hugely. I love that about him. I remember back when he was faking like he was a folk artist, I used to lead him around from gallery to gallery by the hand while he wore torn overalls and kept his glance askance. It was the best borderline-retard impersonation I ever saw: very understated, with his hair looking like a toddler attacked it with kindergarten scissors. Make that a blind toddler.

It was a good act, and his art sold like discounted crack until he himself put a stop to it. It turns out he's a real artist after all, contemporary even. Of course he still wears overalls, just not out in public very much, and his hair is still a wonder to behold. Grant and I enlisted some other passengers to examine it while Daniel slept on the flight from Atlanta, placing bets on whether it was real or not. "Those have got to be plugs," Grant whispered. "No, that's his hair," I insisted. I bet Daniel's secret is that he chops it off in tufts with toenail clippers, then sprinkles his head with cornstarch. His head sort of looks like a moth-eaten ball of horsehair that barely survived a barn fire. For Daniel, it's a very studied effect, one that he won't change even if I promise to pay for it.

"Look, there's a hair salon; get your ass in there for a real haircut," we keep telling him, as L.A. is chockablock with hair salons. Every other doorway boasts an avalanche of hair products. I don't know how Lary can stand it, because of the four of us, he is the one who is a complete pussy about hair care. Nothing touches his head unless

Upward Mobility

it's mint scented and tested by a team of Vietnamese scientists, which is alarming considering the rest of him could be covered in egg yolk and axle grease and he couldn't care less. I estimate that, for shampoo alone, Lary spends more than I do for an entire year's worth of bleaching the hell out of my own head.

Anyway, Daniel always refuses the free salon visit. Oh well, he knows who he is. I'm pretty proud of him for marching into that L.A. gallery with his head looking like it'd been assaulted by bobcats, and then walking out with representation. His new work reminds me of Western Atomic Age, anyway, the kind of stuff my mother used to buy in the early '60s. She had good taste back then. Then all of a sudden in the '70s and early '80s, when she was making decent money designing weapons during the Reagan administration, she went all rattan on us. Our entire condo looked like the movie set of *Casablanca,* complete with bamboo beads hanging in the doorway and dead palm fronds stapled to the walls.

Of course it did not help, at all, that I encouraged her. I'd taken an interior-design course at the local community college and came out insisting that the "Mediterranean look" was in. So the first thing I did was talk her into ejecting all her sleek, teak, '60s Lane furniture she'd had since her honeymoon and replacing it with a bunch of baled bamboo stalks that barely passed as patio furniture. The only regret I remember her voicing was when I'd told her how much I'd gotten for all her old furniture at the garage sale we'd advertised in the local paper. "Twenty-five dollars?" she'd asked, disbelieving. "Is that all? That stuff was valuable. What are those people, blind?"

I was surprised at her reaction. I didn't think she'd mind. But looking back I see I should have known. By then we'd moved twenty-five times; that's twenty-five times we'd packed and unpacked this furniture up and down the California coast, twenty-five times we'd situated it in a welcoming manner throughout another rented living room, twenty-five opportunities for me to realize its value. I didn't tell her that I actually threw this furniture at the people, begged them to buy it, and cut the price so low they couldn't say no. I couldn't wait to replace what I had, which, of course, made me blind to its value.

Daniel's new L.A. gallery has select pieces of furniture from the Eames era interspersed throughout the space, showcased like the marvels in design that they are. Some of them could have actually come from my mother's living room for all I know, as we didn't live far from here when I'd helped catapult these classics out of our lives. I'd love to get them back, of course, but I inevitably wonder what, exactly, I'm hoping to re-create—my old living room or my old life. In either case it's impossible. In either case the pursuit deflects from what I do have—an exacerbating life full of accidents, some happy and some not-so, that led the four of us here to L.A. to sell a television show—so I try not to be so quick to catapult things from my life anymore. I try not to be so blind to their value.

Upward Mobility

What's Stopping Me

///

I CANNOT BELIEVE LARY DIDN'T GET A MEXICAN vasectomy when he had the chance. He and Grant had already ditched Daniel in San Diego on their way to Tijuana, and Grant was off in some skank-ass Latin gay bar with his hands down a Mexican man's pants, so it's not like those two were there to hold Lary back or anything, not that they would.

"You're right there," I said. He'd called me while standing there right outside the clinic; if I was next to him, I'd have pushed him inside. "*What's stopping you?*"

"A flesh-eating staph infection," he answered.

Firm in my conviction that not everyone should propagate, I responded, "Get yer ass in that clinic, or I'll castrate you myself."

To be fair, though, Lary did not go to Tijuana to get a vasectomy, he went there to get drugs—your basic assload of pain relievers, antipsychotics, and other generic-brand mood-morphing substances. The big bag of inhalers, like the possible vasectomy, was an impulse purchase, as was the other asthma medication. Not that any of them have asthma. Lary's cancer-stricken friend, the one from whom Lary usually procures his drugs, has either passed away or, worse, passed so far into the realm of present-day depleted medical care that he can no longer afford to share his drug supply with Lary. So Lary decided to take things into his own hands with the Tijuana drugstore drill.

The side trip to Tijuana was an impulse in itself, as it was the only way I could talk Lary into coming to California with us. For months

I'd planned to storm Hollywood studios regarding an idea for a new series, and Jesus Christ wouldn't you know they, like, *let me in.* They scheduled me some actual goddamn appointments! The first thing I did was call Lary. I cannot possibly go to Hollywood for a meeting with television executives without bringing Lary and the rest of the boys to properly pollinate the air with their craziness molecules. "What's your fucking credit card number?" I yelled when he finally picked up the phone, as I'd already pulled up the airline Web site. But it wasn't until I suggested the Tijuana drug drill that Lary finally coughed up his account information. Daniel, of course, didn't hesitate. The boy is more broke than a beggar in Bangladesh, but credit companies keep sending him cards.

The day after we got to California, everybody scattered like freshly hatched spiders. The first thing those three did was ditch me in Hollywood, but to be fair I guess they had no choice, seeing as how I had those meetings and all. Then they took my rental car and headed for the border. When they called me a few hours later, drunk and screaming from inside a Tijuana cantina, I asked them to please pass the phone to someone sober. "Put Daniel on the line," I said, spending a patient moment of silence gazing at Milly's photo on my cell phone.

And then they told me they'd ditched Daniel in San Diego.

Crap, I thought, because between those three, Daniel is the only one with a legitimate need for prescription drugs. So I hung up on Lary and called Daniel, who was sitting under a tree in Balboa Park, all serene and perfectly trusting in his belief that Grant and Lary would come back for him. I put my head in my hands and wished I'd

Upward Mobility

accepted that handful of generic Valium my flight-attendant friend offered me after her trip to Lima last month.

Because, seriously, I'm amazed I don't do drugs. I'm amazed I don't just soak in a Jacuzzi of narcotics every night. When I was in college, it certainly seemed I was headed that direction, but then college itself is what stopped me when I realized I couldn't afford my tuition if I continued to blow my earnings on blow. Then after college, what stopped me was my airline job, since the easiest way to pass a drug test was to not take drugs.

Now here I was talking to Lary again, this time as he stood outside a Tijuana clinic wondering if he should get a quickie vasectomy while he waits for Grant to finish groping Mexicans. "What's stopping you?" I asked again.

"What's stopping *you*?" he countered, referring to the drugs. "You always have some excuse."

Sugar is my drug of choice these days—and I can proudly say there have been whole periods that lasted almost entire weekends when I don't touch the stuff.

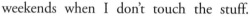

Alcohol is a much more fun addiction— you get to have indiscriminant sex as a side effect and everything—while sugar is just . . . sugar. People feed it to their kids, for chrissakes.

So here I was, no longer being regularly drug tested, and I thought for one gleeful moment that maybe I could test my toe in those waters again. Maybe I *will* snork a couple of bong

bowls when the boys get back. Then we can all lie around laughing until we cough up our own shoes. Why not?

But as I was about to say this to Lary, I saw Milly's picture again, right there on my cell phone.

It made me think of a time not too long ago in Atlanta when I was late to lunch again, which was no big surprise. Grant and Lary always acted affronted by this, as if I was applying for a job with them rather than showing up for my normal dose of denigration. They should be more like Daniel, I say, whose practice is to just go about lunch as though he didn't have a date with me at all; then when I finally do appear, he's super happy to see me. "Why can't you two blowfish be more like Daniel?" I griped as I sat down, which gave them the cue to rise as though lunch were over.

"At least you made it in time to say goodbye," Grant quipped, rising to leave.

"Sit down, Lord Jesus God," I hollered, and they did, but not because I begged them to. The real reason is because there was still a drop or two left in their cocktail glasses. "I'm sorry I'm late," I sighed, "The city is laying new roads and the asphalt is all torn up like pork chops after a pit-bull attack."

This is not the real reason, but one that will do. The real reason is that I spent the morning rummaging through my closet to find clothes to fit my mom-body, something these two cinder blocks will never understand. By the time I finished wailing and got dressed, I was so late for lunch that the kitchen was closed and Lary had to begrudgingly let me nibble on his leftovers. Not that he wanted them for himself. No,

Upward Mobility

the real reason is he likes to take any opportunity to point out that, unlike me, he has not gained one single pound since we met fifteen years ago.

"Look, loser," I tell him, "when I want to sign up for the Lary Blodgett coffee-enema-and-Internet-amphetamine diet, I'll make sure to tell you so we can shop for matching hospital gowns. But for now I'd like to live, so fork over the tuna roll, turdball."

"Bitch, have a cocktail," Grant insisted. It's been years since I quit drinking, but Grant acts like this is just a phase, as though it's just a matter of catching me in the right mood and I'll have my shirt open demanding people suck body shots off my hooters like half his customers at closing time. I think it must be because my drinking didn't go out with a bang. There was no DUI or twelve-step program or regrettable binge when I woke up in bed with three bullwhips and a colostomy bag or anything. I simply lost my taste for alcohol one day and stopped drinking it, that's all.

Of course, though all that is true, it's not the real reason. Whenever I try to explain the real reason to these guys, they wave me off like an annoying gnat. Maybe Grant does get it a little, because he's a parent and sometimes I think he understands. Because the real reason I don't drink is because I have a kid now, and I have already made things hard enough by publishing a book with the word "Bitch" in the title, which, let's face it, revels in the debauchery of my youth. All it took was one verbally abusive parent at my daughter's preschool, armed with a complete inability to put things in proper context, and before I knew it my girl and I were ostracized to playdate wasteland.

Now, as I've always told Milly, "Judgment is more revealing of the person passing it than the person receiving it." But that's not a lot of comfort to a kid when the other kids can't come over because their parents have been told her mom is a wild partier. Maybe I could have stood on principle and ended my abstinence to drink moderately like the other parents, but all I know is that my principles can't climb the monkey bars with my kid. So I wish I could give you a super colorful reason for why I don't drink—like how I woke up in jail in a puddle of some post-op tranny prostitute's vomit or something, but that is not the real reason.

"C'mon, have a margarita," Grant joked.

"Can't. Gotta work," I said. Again, not the real reason, but one that would do.

Now the boys are down in Mexico, or scattered in that direction, anyway, beckoning me to party with them, and I have to admit it's tempting. My girl is safe somewhere else, cared for by family members so I could be free to make this sojourn back to my California roots on the wave of my success; what better way to celebrate the full circle than to revel a little in the same debauchery that made up most of the material that got me here?

"What's stopping you?" Lary asked again, hollering over the mariachi music in the background. "You better pick up Daniel on your way back," I told Lary instead, "or I'll personally rip out your kidneys."

At that I hung up but kept the phone open and gazed at Milly's face. When I look at her face, I practically want to fall over backward and fling my arms out with pride. Her face. Her little face. It is so unfailingly dear to me it stops my breath, among other things.

Upward Mobility

Mr. Big Smile

//

THE NEXT TIME GRANT ASKS YOU TO SNIFF HIS HAND, I'd advise against it. We were at the Beverly Laurel Motor Hotel in West Hollywood (because you can get four rooms there in exchange for the one that was booked for me at the Beverly Hilton), and Grant was sitting on my bed, going on about how he plans on moving to Tijuana because so many Mexicans live there—"and I do love me some Mexican man meat," he laughed his big-smile laugh—and up went his hand to his face again. He just kept *sniffing his hand.*

"Why the hell are you sniffing your hand?" I asked.

"He's been doing that since he left the gay bar in Tijuana," Lary said. Lary, by the way, regrettably opted out of the impromptu vasectomy offered by a perfectly passable south-of-the-border clinic with hardly any *E. coli* encrusted on the surgical instruments or anything (probably), a move that confounded me, because it's just unlike Lary not to take advantage of an opportunity.

Anyway, now Grant refuses to wash his right hand because that was the one he used to grope all the cute little Latin "love monkeys" the whole time he was in Tijuana. In the other hand he held his margarita, because, of course, one must have priorities. Eventually Lary lassoed Grant's roving hand and forced him to leave the bar. I can't see Lary ever being the voice of reason, but since he isn't gay I'm sure he got tired of being aggressively groped by those who were while he waited for Grant to finish soaking in a sea of hedonism. "They were jumping all over me," Lary complained of the other patrons. "I almost spilled my margarita."

"Smell my hand!" Grant demanded as he lay sprawled on my bedspread.

"Get the hell off my bed," I said, and I tried to kick him out of my room, but he kept spreading his arms out like a caught lobster so he couldn't fit through the doorway. "Smell my hand! Smell my hand!"

"Get *out!*" I wailed, but horribly, he refused. So I turned around, balled up the bedspread, and threw it on the balcony. Does he not *know* I once lived with my mother in a trailer two miles north of the Tijuana border? I've heard the stories! True, real-life actual stories, like the time my friend once caught crabs just by sitting in a booth at a Tijuana brothel drinking beer while waiting for his friend to finish hosing a hooker upstairs. I remember he said he didn't think it was fair that he caught crabs just for sitting in a booth and behaving, but back home he was having an affair with his next-door neighbor's girlfriend, which I wouldn't exactly call behaving, and in the end he passed the crabs to her and it busted them both.

Also, there was the story, actually true, I swear, of the Texas college kid who went to a rough border town to party with his friends and ended up as human chum in a satanic ritual.

Anyway, that is not the point, as it seemed that Lary and Grant, along with Daniel, made it back safely from Tijuana, thank God. So I guess the point is this: Of the three meetings I had scheduled with the production studio, one of these guys was supposed to attend two with me, starting the next morning. That's right, it had been requested by the execs that I pick one representative from this band of blowfish to come in with me so they could "see the chemistry," so I've been thinking about how Daniel cuts his hair himself with toenail clippers (which might actually be a plus) and Lary is such an evil, fermented alley cat I'm certain he'd take hostages right after the introductions were made (another possible plus).

But of the four of us, Grant is the salesman. He can sell bloody Band-Aids to a germaphobe, I swear. "Jesus God," I gasped as I realized that, of all the people I can choose to go in there with me to present my life's work—just years of me opening an artery every week is all, just my latest hope of having any semblance of security now that my blue-collar day job got flushed by corporate pork, and my house has been under contract four times and still sits there unsold is all— of all the people I could pick to go in there with me, *my best option is Grant.* Grant! Mr. Salesman. Mr. Big Smile. Mr. Smell-My-Hand man. I put my head in my palms and tried to monitor my breathing.

Daniel, Grant, and Lary had dissipated to the balcony, and I could hear them discussing the possibility of stealing the motel's big neon sign. As the sun set behind the Hollywood Hills, they pointed out their favorite homes in the distance along Laurel Canyon as though these mansions were waiting there to be plucked like truffles from a giant chocolate box. Grant, of course, was sniffing his hand again.

"Please wash your hand before tomorrow!" I begged.

Grant just held his hand aloft and laughed his big-smile laugh. "I ain't never washing it again!" he shouted.

Well Packed

///

LARY'S IN MEXICO AGAIN, PROBABLY DEAD IN THE GUTTER from some bionic skanky-hooker syphilis for all I know, which would really piss me off because I have this contract in my hand he needs to sign. We just sold the film rights to my book to a major studio for a major television series. We also somehow got a major producer attached, as well as a major show runner to head the writing team, not to mention a major movie star to agree to play the lead character—everything was so *major!*

"Has Lary called you or e-mailed you or anything?" I ask Grant, who himself is in goddamn New York City pounding on doors to put together his own book deal, never mind that he hasn't written any actual pages or anything ("But I've got a *concept,*" he keeps saying). They act as if they have no idea they're supposed to be my peeps. They just keep flitting about in their own worlds, pretending like they have a life without me. At least Grant, though, signed the contract for his life rights before he disappeared, signed it that day and overnighted it back to the studio. He also whored himself in as a consultant on the future series. (The first thing he plans to do is audition to play himself, and I cannot wait for the day he's turned down for *that* role.)

Daniel, now, is a total free radical. You just never know how he's gonna flow. He and his boyfriend, Mitch, just bought a house off Chamblee-Tucker. The biggest perk is that Daniel now has uber-cable television. When a producer from Paramount came to visit us last

May to wine and dine us, Daniel made some excuse to get out of it, like he needed to pack or something, when he must have known none of us would buy that because we know Daniel doesn't pack. He just leaves everything behind.

Take when Daniel changed studio space. The property manager there e-mailed me to politely inquire as to why Daniel left every bit of everything still sitting there, all his artwork and everything, left behind. The only thing Daniel removed at the end of his lease was himself, and maybe the hair dryer he used to seal the cement he sometimes employed in his pieces. So of course it couldn't be because Daniel had to pack that he was avoiding us, and we were starting to wonder if he was mad at us until we realized that here it was the day of the QVC Suzanne Somers marathon.

After that, Grant pretty much dragged Daniel out of his place. "You fag," he laughed, "just tape the thing."

"I don't know how to use my DVD recorder. I don't know anyone who knows how to use theirs," Daniel protested, and I totally understand that.

When I was on *The Tonight Show with Jay Leno*, not a single one of my techno-retard friends taped it and neither did I. It fell to my old friend Bob Steed, who is a partner at a huge law firm and really should have better ways to waste his time, to track down a DVD for me. Today, I keep it in a drawer all by itself. It's a hallowed thing, the DVD of me on *Jay Leno*. I'm wearing a vintage early '60s turquoise-blue cocktail suit Grant bought at a thrift store for $25 that afternoon. Back at the hotel, I had tried it on but I didn't think I'd wear it because

I'd already maxed out my credit card with the new outfit I bought the week before.

"Bitch, you are wearing the blue suit," he growled at me, and I did, more because I didn't have time to take it off before I ended up onstage. Because, I swear to God, things go fast. It's still hard to believe that we were just that morning trolling all the thrift stores on La Brea after having flown in from Atlanta. Then came our third trip to L.A.

Regarding our flight there, most everyone knows that I am, of course, a master packer. I brag about it so much that Daniel, Grant, and Lary only travel with me on the condition I won't lecture them on the correct technique, which mystifies me because why would you resent the good-intended advice of a friend when it comes to a well-packed suitcase?

"Jesus God! What is that?" I shrieked at Grant when I picked him up on the way to our plane. He had stuffed his orange '70s Samsonite with probably a gajillion different outfits to choose from for our meetings the next day, including his DayGlo prison jumper the color of traffic cones.

"Shut up, bitch," he shrieked back.

"Seriously, I'm embarrassed to be seen with you," I said, and that's saying something, because I have proudly walked into hoity-toity art-gallery openings on Grant's arm while he wore his slinky black side-split "man skirt" with his big head decked out in two 'fro-puff pigtails. But this now, this is what he calls packing?

Upward Mobility

"I said, shut up, bitch," Grant repeated, "and help me lift this into the car."

I rolled my eyes and nearly broke my spine doing as he asked. Standing beside him at the airport, I simply wanted to curdle into a crawling pool of pure mortification, as just my proximity to Grant's suitcase cast a pall over all the proud years I spent as an airline scullery plebe. This exalted past is how I learned to pack with the efficiency of an orphanage warden. Seriously, I can fit the contents of your grandmother's attic into a standard carry-on, and I am not exaggerating much.

The secret to a well-packed suitcase lies in understanding the line that separates the essential from the nonessential—very important, because it is an undeniable fact that people think they need more than they really need. So with this in mind, before a trip I usually assess everything I'm certain I can't live without—such as my electric percolator and my collection of propane-powered curling irons—then I cut that pile in half, then I pack half of that, and even then I always have twice as much as I need, especially if I am traveling with a baggage sherpa like Grant, who brings his own specialty lavender-and-mint shampoo even though the small bottle of dish-soap grade battery acid the motel leaves for you in the shower works fine.

"Lemme borrow some of that super-wuss, $100-shit shampoo," I yelled at Grant from our bathroom at the Beverly Laurel Motor Hotel. We shared a room this time, after I made Grant promise not to drag back any Mexican busboys to spend the night. Grant goes a little crazy in L.A., due to its closeness to Mexico coupled with Grant's famous hankering for Latin men.

"Bitch, get your grubby-ass hands out of my suitcase," Grant said.

Later, in the parking lot before driving to our appointment at the Warner Bros. lot, I paused. All of a sudden it hit me, what we had accomplished so far. I turned to Grant and beamed. "Here we are," I squealed. "Here we are, here we are, here we are!"

"Calm down," Grant soothed me. "Look at me."

He took my hand and commanded my gaze with those blue eyes like two turquoise medallions in the middle of his big, freckly-assed face. We were in a rented PT Cruiser again, which turned out to be the sole model available at the cheapest rental-car company in LAX, which I thought was hilarious because Grant famously loathes my PT Cruiser back home. Yet here he was holding my hand in one right outside our motel as we were about to head to our most-important meeting so far.

So I was looking at him like he told me to, and I was expecting him to say something. But he didn't. He just kept holding my hand and looking back at me with that expression he has—the one that says, "I got no job, no dreams, no aspirations; I'm the happiest man alive"—until all of a sudden it hit me: the line that separates the essential from the nonessential. Right then I could see it as clear as day. Television series or no, my life was well packed.

Upward Mobility

Flotation Device

ON THE WAY HOME IT OCCURRED TO ME that if my plane crashed into the ocean, I doubt my seat cushion would save me, but you never know. I'm not that picky or proud about things that might save me or my daughter. I'll grab at anything.

I know this after having watched the movie *Titanic* twenty-four times, all without sound, since it was playing on a movie screen of an L-1011 during international flights, and as an international flight attendant, I was frowned upon if I plugged my earphones into the armrest to hear it. Believe me, I tried.

I watched it, though, over and over and over again, while serving Cokes and overcooked meat, and I always wondered why the hell didn't those people—the ones who drowned—why the hell didn't they grab onto something? Jesus God, in the time it took that giant ship to sink, those people could have dismantled the paneling in the mezzanine level and built their own damn boat. Just the lid on the grand piano in the dining room alone would have floated a whole family, probably. *Make something, do something!* I kept imploring the poor idiots who were left to die like flies after the ineffectual lifeboats launched without them. *What are you doing standing in line to get on a lifeboat? Look around! Build your own damn boat!*

Milly and I travel a lot together now that I'm a writer and no longer a flight attendant, the difference being—and it's an important difference—that my girl can now come with me on the plane while I work. My new company, which I founded, takes me to tons of places a little girl would love to visit, mostly because I am my own boss and I make sure it does.

On the plane, when we take our assigned seats, the safety placard is usually the first thing Milly reaches for, and I tell her the difference between the oxygen system on this plane as opposed to the last plane we were on. "These masks, we have to yank on 'em a little, see? Because there's that pin—see the pin?—you have to yank that pin loose to activate the oxygen. Don't forget that."

And we count the rows to her closest exits, too. It took her a few times to get that down, because sometimes the closest exits are behind you, and I learned in evacuation training that people tend to run forward in a panic. They don't think to look behind them. Just like with those passengers on the *Titanic*. First they wasted critical time denying the severity of the impact, and then once the crisis was evident, they were so busy crowding forward toward the few lifeboats that they didn't look behind them, where tons of wooden things were begging to be made into makeshift flotation devices. "Look behind you, look to the side of you," I tell Milly. "Don't just be looking where everyone else is looking."

Christ, I hope she'll never have to use this information, but I can't help but think it might come in handy, regardless. Back when I first got hired at the airlines, for example, I figured I'd be working there until they pried the peanuts from my cold, dead fingers. I had no plans to leave. Ever. I wanted to hang on until I was nothing but a withered bit of beef jerky in a work smock, cracking wise with the passengers, ignoring call bells and belting fine wine on European

Upward Mobility

layovers. It was a great job up until the precise moment the first 757 crashed into the World Trade Center. Even before the second plane hit, I knew it was over.

My job didn't sink right away. In fact, it stayed afloat, though crippled, for a deceptively long while after that, long enough to keep my fellow blue-collar coworkers hoping the blow wasn't that catastrophic, long enough to allow first class to board the lifeboats all by themselves. But our jobs were sinking, that's the truth, listing this way and that, and when it finally became evident the ship was going down, that in fact the officers had spent the entire time building a whole other ship for themselves, one that would replace the one that was already lost, that's when the mad dash for the emergency exits began.

Now I've made a lot of mistakes in my life: I married the wrong man. I've turned down perfectly good, guilt-free sex with B-list celebrities. I wasn't at my father's side, where I rightfully should have been, when he died without warning one night. But once you become a mother, you have to figure it out. It's not as though you can no longer afford to make mistakes; it's just that you can no longer afford not to learn from them.

So when the first plane hit the World Trade Center, I wasn't going to make the mistake of denying the severity of the impact. I immediately started looking around for things that could keep me afloat. I looked beside me, I looked behind me, I especially looked where others weren't looking. I didn't find any one thing that would work on its own, but I'm not that picky or proud about things that might save me or my daughter. I grabbed at anything—freelance assignments, my humor column in the local weekly—and found a lot I could cobble together, so that by the time others were mobbing the ineffectual lifeboats, I had already built, rickety as it was, my own makeshift flotation device.

Upward Mobility

The Checklist

LARY IS THE LAST PERSON WHO SHOULD BE HERE. I need help, I tell you. *Help*. I need someone to hold me back, not someone to *back me up*, because right now, as I speak, there is already, erected in my backyard, a haunted house that is bigger than the house I actually live in. That right there is evidence I have a problem. Last year I was able to rein it in a little, even though I built a canopy to cover my front yard in case it rained—which of course it so *totally* did—so thank God for that, but my snack selection was so huge I might as well have set the kids loose in the candy aisle at Wal-Mart. By the time they got home, they were probably so coked up they could set off seismic monitors stationed in the arctic. (You're welcome, parents.)

This year is already amounting to the mother of all Halloween parties. I have all this time on my hands seeing as how, two days after we closed that television rights deal, a writer's strike shut down Hollywood. To distract myself I paid five guys to clear the giant morass of thorn bushes that formerly made up my backyard so that now there is actually room to walk back there, though it is still not accessible by trailer, so mine still sit in my driveway out front, festooned with giant spiders and other Halloween essentials. Clearing the backyard is a good first step toward eventually moving them back there, though, but it was like excavating, I swear. I actually uncovered a windmill, for chrissakes, and a frame for a swing set. Who knew? I was half relieved we didn't find a set of little mummified tykes to go with it, still sitting in the swings.

"That would have been cool," said Lary.

TRAILER TRASHED

262

Like I said, Lary is the last person who should be here. After all, Lary is a rigger for large-scale events. People actually pay him to take their crazy-assed party ideas and make them a reality. This explains why, a few years ago, when I asked him to help me decorate Milly's fourth-birthday party, the theme for which was "Castle Princess," he showed up with a rented bulldozer to dig a moat.

Lary is hanging outdoor speakers so the sounds of tortured groans can be carried throughout my backyard. "If you don't want to kill any kids," he says, "you should use the heavier wire." I would very much like not to electrocute my guests, no matter how much Lary insists that fried people would provide cool Halloween props, so I opted for the heavier wire. Earlier I'd had him on the phone at Home Depot, trying to collect all the spooled coils and clip sockets and other electrical components he said were essential to activate the animatrons set up in one of my trailers, which had been converted into a haunted autopsy morgue, when all of a sudden it occurred to me what the hell it was, exactly, that Lary was aiming to get me to make.

"This sounds like an *extension cord!* Are we *making* an extension cord?" I hissed. "You retard! I can buy them for a buck a piece at Family Dollar!"

"Sure," he said, "but what's the fun in that?"

Lord, I do not have time to build my own extension cords. I have important things to do. I have a checklist. Do I have enough fake blood? Check. Did I remember to buy the foam board for the fake tombstones? Check. Did I borrow the rubber carcass from my neighbor? Check.

Upward Mobility

Before Milly, all this energy used to go into my own costume, which often included blinking lights and battery packs. One year I was so exhausted after getting into costume that I sat down to rest before hitting the parties, only to awaken on my couch four hours later with the illuminated skull on the end of my scepter barely still glowing.

Now I let Milly pick our costumes. She's old enough now to ask for less bizarre stuff, like this year she simply asked that I be a witch like her. I expected to feel more relieved than I was, but instead the feeling was clouded by an odd melancholy. "I still have the double-butted baboon costume from last year," I offered meekly, but she demurred, even going so far as to suggest that the baboon butts were not *National Geographic* grade.

What? Last year that costume garnered me God status in Milly's eyes. She showed me off to her classmates like a prized captured spider, and my heart shot like a rocket right out of my chest. Realizing now that the double-butted baboon costume has lost all its power makes me want to groan like the torture victims on the Halloween sound track.

Instead I look at all the Halloween pictures taken since Milly was born: the ladybug costume at age one, the sparkle princess at two, the mermaid at three, and so on. I look at her face in those photos, and I go over my other checklist. Did I hang her pumpkin drawings? Check. Have I laid out her costume? Check. Does my soul widen like the open sky when I look in her eyes? Do I cry with pride at the sight of her? Does my heart happily break every day she grows and makes her way? Check, check, check.

Acknowledgments

I want to thank Kim and Eddie, Cheryl and Jim, and of course, Daniel, Grant, Lary, and Keiger. My daughter deserves thanks, too, as well as the acknowledgment that she is not fatherless.

Others to whom I owe gratitude are Lynn Lamousin, Suzanne Van Atten, Ken Edelstein, Doug Monroe, David Warner, Carlton Hargro, Besha Rodell and Charles McNair. My gratitude also goes to Jay Leno, Mike Henry, Jolie Ancel, Bob and Lu Steed, Patrick Best, Rebecca Burns, Liz Lapidus, Jackie Mitchard, Karin Slaughter, Tim Dorsey, Jim Hackler, Michael Benoit, Laura Geraci, Thomas Meagher, Jim and Anna Llewellyn, Michael Alvear, Randy Osborne, Polly Biasucci, Amy Paradysz and Himeka Curiel . . . and Dave Barry, for his influence and the fact that I reliably rip the hell off of him.

Finally, a
skirt!
that fits!

www.skirt.com

skirt!®